Basiswortschatz Englisch im Griff

von John Flower

Ernst Klett Verlag für Wissen und Bildung
Stuttgart · Dresden

Basiswortschatz Englisch im Griff

von John Flower
Deutsche Bearbeitung: Axel Ruland

Dieses Symbol  weist auf einen Lerntip hin.

 Gedruckt auf chlorfrei hergestelltem Papier,
säurefrei und ohne optische Aufheller

1. Auflage   1 ⁴ ³ ² ¹ | 1999 98 97 96

© LTP 1995
   Titel der Originalausgabe:
   Start Building Your Vocabulary

Redaktion: Elizabeth Webster
Einbandgestaltung: Ilona Arfaoui
Druck: Druckerei zu Altenburg
Printed in Germany.

ISBN 3-12-560964-X

Inhaltsverzeichnis

1. Kapitel

Start Building Your Vocabulary
Erweitern Sie Ihren Wortschatz

1. Wörter sind die wichtigsten Bestandteile einer Sprache.

Die englische Sprache verfügt über den größten Wortschatz aller Sprachen. Grammatik ist zwar wichtig, aber Wörter sind weitaus wichtiger.

2. Führen Sie ein Vokabelheft.

Notieren Sie die neuen Wörter und Phrasen, die Sie lernen möchten. Organisieren Sie Ihr Vokabelheft in einer Form, die Ihnen ein rasches Auffinden Ihrer Einträge ermöglicht.

3. Dieses Kapitel ist wichtig.

Bearbeiten Sie zunächst dieses Kapitel. Es enthält wertvolle Anregungen zum besseren Lernen.

4. Es fehlt oft die Zeit, viele Wörter zu lernen.

Sie machen die besten Fortschritte, wenn Sie Ihren Wortschatz selbständig erweitern – zu Hause, im Bus, vor dem Fernseher, überall! Auch wenn Sie zur Zeit an einem Englischkurs teilnehmen, werden Sie feststellen, daß es viele Dinge während des Unterrichts zu tun gibt und nur wenig Zeit bleibt, den Wortschatz zu erweitern.

1.1 How to use this book
So benutzen Sie dieses Buch

1. Bearbeiten Sie zunächst dieses Kapitel vollständig.
2. Nach Bearbeitung des 1. Kapitels suchen Sie sich aus den anderen Kapiteln die Übungen aus, die Sie bearbeiten möchten – nach Ihrem Belieben und in der von Ihnen gewünschten Reihenfolge.
3. Am Schluß befinden sich fünf Tests, mit denen Sie Ihre Fortschritte gleich messen können.
4. Zur optimalen Arbeit mit diesem Buch benötigen Sie zwei Dinge:
   – ein gutes Wörterbuch und ein Vokabelheft
5. Benutzen Sie Ihr Vokabelheft möglichst jeden Tag zum Eintragen von Begriffen, die Ihnen wichtig erscheinen.

1.2 Some important words
Einige wichtige Wörter

Die Wörter auf der linken Seite unten werden zu Beginn dieses Buches häufig verwendet. Ordnen Sie sie den Phrasen auf der rechten Seite zu. Tragen Sie Ihre Antworten in die Kästchen unterhalb der Übung ein. Einige sind schon für Sie eingetragen worden.

1.	verb	a.	I'll meet you **at** the corner.
2.	noun	b.	We've got a **cat**.
3.	pronunciation	c.	I never **eat** meat.
4.	phonetic symbols	d.	It's as easy as **ABC**.
5.	phrase	e.	We only have a **small** car.
6.	adjective	f.	The sound of a word.
7.	preposition	g.	nation = [neɪʃən]
8.	phrasal verb	h.	It's late! **Hurry up!**
9.	capital letters	i.	We leave **in the morning**.

1.	2.	3. *f.*	4. *g.*	5.	6.	7. *a.*	8. *h.*	9.

1.3 Find the right word
Finden Sie das richtige Wort

Schlagen Sie die folgenden Wörter in Ihrem Wörterbuch nach. Welche zwei Wörter kann man im Zusammenhang mit einer Busfahrt benutzen?

answer   catch   example   fare   vowel

1.4 Word partnerships
Wortpartnerschaften

Wenn Sie ein Wort im Wörterbuch nachschlagen, schauen Sie sich die dortigen Verwendungsbeispiele an. Welche anderen Wörter werden häufig im Zusammenhang mit diesem Wort benutzt?

Ordnen Sie den Verben in der linken Spalte ein Nomen der rechten Spalte zu. Benutzen Sie jedes Wort nur einmal. Schreiben Sie die Wörter zusammen auf. Beispiel:

1. speak	a bath	*speak English* . . . . .
2. do	a bike	. . . .
3. have	a bus	. . . .
4. make	English	. . . .
5. play	TV	. . . .
6. ride	your homework	. . . .
7. catch	a mistake	. . . .
8. watch	golf	. . . .

Nehmen Sie nun einige Ihrer Antworten zur Vervollständigung folgender Sätze.

9. You can . . . . from the stop outside the station.

10. Does Eva . . . . ?   > She only knows a few words.

11. What's your favourite sport?   > I often . . . . but I prefer football.

12. Do you . . . . very much?   > Not really. Most of the programmes are so stupid!

1.5 Word families
Wortfamilien

Wenn Sie ein Wort im Wörterbuch gefunden haben, versuchen Sie daraus andere Wörter abzuleiten, wie zum Beispiel:

information → inform   use → useful → useless

Verändern Sie die Wörter am Ende der Sätze, um diese zu vervollständigen.

1. I like it here. Everybody's so . . . . . *friendly* . . . . (FRIEND)
2. If the sea is too cold, you can use the . . . . .pool. (SWIM)
3. Don't walk on the road! It's very . . . . ! (DANGER)
4. On her wall she has a copy of a . . . . by Dalí. (PAINT)
5. Have you got any . . . . about your English classes? (INFORM)
6. I don't want to go out. It's so cold and . . . . ! (WIND)

1.6 Pronunciation
Aussprache

Wörterbücher benutzen phonetische Symbole, um die Aussprache der Begriffe zu beschreiben. Wenn Sie sich diese Symbole einprägen, werden Sie immer die Aussprache eines Begriffs bestimmen können.

In der folgenden Liste finden Sie Wörter mit drei verschiedenen Aussprachen des Buchstaben „o". Tragen Sie die Wörter in die entsprechende Gruppe ein.

brother	close	come	copy	front	g̶o̶
home	h̶o̶t̶	job	long	love	money
most	often	o̶n̶e̶	open	show	stop

1. [ʌ]	2. [ɒ]	3. [əʊ]
one	*hot*	*go* . . . .
. . . .	. . . .	. . . .
. . . .	. . . .	. . . .
. . . .	. . . .	. . . .
. . . .	. . . .	. . . .
. . . .	. . . .	. . . .

1.7 Words in sentences
Wörter in Sätzen

Wenn Sie neue Wörter in Ihr Vokabelheft eintragen, ist es empfehlenswert, einen Beispielsatz aufzuschreiben. Dadurch werden Sie sich leichter an das Wort erinnern und können sich seine Bedeutung besser einprägen.

Tragen Sie die folgenden Wörter an der richtigen Stelle ein, und fügen Sie hinzu, was Ihnen hilft, das Wort besser zu lernen, z. B. die Übersetzung des Begriffs ins Deutsche.

artist	delicious	department store	give up	hurry
of course	out of order	recommend	shampoo	terrible

1. *hurry* . . . . . = **go quickly**

   I must . *hurry* . . . or I'll be late for work.

2. . . . . = **good to eat**

   Can I have some more, please. This is . . . .

3. . . . . = **somebody who paints pictures**

   Salvador Dalí is Helen's favourite . . . .

4. . . . . = **certainly/yes**

   Can I have something to drink? < . . . . you can.

5. . . . . = **stop**

   You must . . . . smoking! You know it's bad for you!

6. . . . . = **big shop selling many different things**

   You can buy almost anything you want in this . . . .

7. . . . . = **very bad**

   The weather is . . . . ! It's very cold and wet.

8. . . . . = **not working**

   I can't use the phone. It's . . . .

9. . . . . = **tell someone that something is good**

   I don't know any good restaurants. Can you . . . . one?

10. . . . . = **a liquid for washing your hair**

    This new . . . . washes my hair much better.

9

1.8 **Words from texts**
Wörter aus Texten

Wenn Sie einen englischen Text gelesen haben, sollte Sie ihn noch einmal lesen und nach nützlichen Wörtern und Wortverbindungen suchen. Achten Sie dabei nicht auf einzelne Wörter, sondern schauen Sie sich den Zusammenhang an, in dem sie stehen.

Lesen Sie den Text. Unterstreichen Sie alle Wörter und Wortverbindungen, die für Sie nützlich sind.

A Traveller's Story

I hate flying. It's the worst way to travel. First of all, your plane leaves at 10 o'clock in the morning. Fine. But you have to be there at 8. You live 50 miles from the airport. So, you leave home at 6. That means getting up at 5. Crazy!

You don't want to be late, so you take a taxi. The trains are terrible, but the traffic is awful! You sit in a traffic jam for 45 minutes. Are you going to miss your plane?

No. You arrive just in time. But now you stand in a queue at the check-in for another half an hour. In front of you is a noisy family of eight and an elderly couple who can't find their passports. Then you stand in another queue at passport control for 15 minutes. You are not happy!

Finally, you go through passport control. You have exactly 8 minutes to buy something from the duty-free shop before it's time to board the plane. Then you have a long journey in front of you. The seats are very small. The person sitting next to you is very fat. He wants to tell you his life story . . . .

That's what normally happens. But yesterday it was different. Yesterday the person sitting next to me on the plane was a tall, thin man with long black hair and dark glasses. He didn't say a word to me for over an hour. When the flight attendant brought drinks, he refused. When she brought lunch, he refused again.

Suddenly, the man stood up. He took something out of his travel bag. It was a gun. People started to scream. The flight attendant came over to us.

"Can I help you, sir?" she asked.

"Take me to Havana – or I'll blow the plane up!"

The flight attendant smiled.

"Please sit down, sir. Havana's where we're going. Now, what would you like to drink?"

Übung

Schauen Sie sich die folgenden Wortverbindungen aus dem Text an. Tragen Sie die fehlenden Wörter ein. Ein Beispiel ist vorgegeben.

1. Nomen + Nomen

  traffic jam . . . . . . control . . . . . . attendant . . . . . . bag

2. Verb + Nomen

  . . . . . . home . . . . . . a taxi . . . . . . your plane . . . . . . the plane

3. Verb + Präposition + Nomen

  You stand . . . . a queue.

  You go . . . . passport control.

  You buy something . . . . the duty-free shop.

4. Zeitbegriffe

  Your plane leaves . . . . 10 o'clock . . . . the morning.

  You sit in a traffic jam . . . . 45 minutes.

5. Allgemeine Adjektive

  A tall, thin . . . . with long black . . . . and dark

  . . . .

6. Verb-Präposition-Verbindungen

  You leave home at 6. That means getting . . . . at 5!

  Suddenly, the man stood . . . .

  "Take me to Havana or I'll blow the plane . . . . !"

7. Nützliche Ausdrücke

  " . . . . I help you?"

  "Please sit . . . ."

  "What would you . . . . to drink?"

8. Tragen Sie hier andere nützliche Wörter und Ausdrücke ein, die Sie im Text gefunden haben.

  . . . .

  . . . .

  . . . .

1.9 Words from pictures
Wörter aus Bildern

Auch mit Hilfe von Bildern kann man sich Wörter einprägen! Verschiedene Übungen in diesem Buch verwenden Bilder. Sie können sich aber auch Ihr persönliches Bild-Wörterbuch zusammenstellen. Sie können Bilder aus Zeitschriften ausschneiden oder auch selbst zeichnen. Dazu muß man nicht unbedingt künstlerisch begabt sein.

Schreiben Sie die folgenden 12 Phrasen unter das jeweils passende Bild.

short and fat	tall and thin	thin and bald	old and poor
young and happy	wet and windy	nice and sunny	tired and dirty
tired and sleepy	rich and famous	hot and angry	nice and tasty

1. . . . .
2. . . . .
3. . . . .
4. . . . .
5. . . . .
6. . . . .
7. . . . .
8. . . . .
9. . . . .
10. . . . .
11. . . . .
12. . . . .

2. Kapitel

Word Groups
Wortgruppen

1. Lernen Sie die Wörter in Gruppen.

Die englische Sprache verfügt über einen fast unerschöpflichen Wortschatz. Versuchen Sie daher, Wörter in Gruppen zu lernen. Zum Beispiel:

- Wörter für Kleidungsstücke

- Wörter für Berufe

- Wörter für Hobbys

2. Stellen Sie Wortgruppen in Ihrem Vokabelheft zusammen.

In diesem Kapitel sollen Sie erstmals Wörter in Gruppen zusammenfassen. Sie können, wenn Sie möchten, Ihre Übersetzung neben jedes Wort einer Gruppe schreiben.

Der persönliche Wortschatz läßt sich erweitern, indem man zu einem bestimmten Thema alle Wörter, die einem einfallen, aufschreibt. Diese Listen können dann jederzeit mit neuen Wörtern erweitert werden.

In der folgenden Übung finden Sie Wörter aus vier verschiedenen Themenbereichen. Tragen Sie sie in die entsprechende Liste ein und schreiben Sie die Themen darüber.

armchair	concert	opera singer	stool
bed	cousin	parents	table
brother-in-law	drums	play a tune	uncle
black	grandson	pop song	violin
blue	green	red	white
chair	nephew	sofa	yellow

1.	2. *family*	3.	4. . . . .
armchair	*brother-in-law*	*black*	*concert*

Kennen Sie noch andere Wörter, die Sie den einzelnen Themen hinzufügen können?

Word groups (2) – sport, drinks, clothes, weather

Wortgruppen (2) – Sport, Getränke, Kleidung, Wetter

Tragen Sie diese Wörter in eine der vier Spalten ein und schreiben Sie die Themen darüber.

baseball team	heavy rain	pair of socks	sunny
bottle of wine	lemonade	pair of trousers	sunshine
blouse	long skirt	play volleyball	tennis court
cup of coffee	temperature	referee	warm coat
football stadium	mineral water	shower	win the match
glass of milk	orange juice	smart suit	windy

1.	2.	3.	4. . . . .
baseball team	*bottle of wine*	*blouse*	*heavy rain*

Kennen Sie noch andere Wörter, die Sie den einzelnen Themen hinzufügen können?

Days, months, seasons
Wochentage, Monate, Jahreszeiten

Tragen Sie diese Begriffe in der korrekten Reihenfolge in die entsprechenden Listen ein.

afternoon	February	May	October	Thursday
April	Friday	minute	Saturday	Tuesday
August	hour	Monday	second	Wednesday
autumn	January	month	September	week
day	July	morning	spring	winter
December	June	night	summer	year
evening	March	November	Sunday	

Days

1. *Monday*

2. . . . .

3. . . . .

4. . . . .

5. . . . .

6. . . . .

7. . . . .

Parts of a day

1. *morning*

2. . . . .

3. . . . .

4. . . . .

Months

1. *January*

2. . . . .

3. . . . .

4. . . . .

5. . . . .

6. . . . .

7. . . . .

8. . . . .

9. . . . .

10. . . . .

11. . . . .

12. . . . .

Seasons

1. *spring*

2. . . . .

3. . . . .

4. . . . .

Time

1. *second*

2. . . . .

3. . . . .

4. . . . .

5. . . . .

6. . . . .

7. . . . .

 Bitte beachten Sie, daß Wochentage und Monatsnamen im Englischen mit einem Großbuchstaben beginnen.

2.4 Men and women
Männer und Frauen

Wenn wir Nomen benutzen, um über Männer und Frauen zu sprechen, benutzen wir gewöhnlich für beide Geschlechter das gleiche Wort, z. B.:

> *doctor, cousin, student*

Es gibt aber auch manchmal zwei unterschiedliche Wörter, z. B.:

> *son, daughter*

Tragen Sie die folgenden Wörter in die entsprechende Spalte der Tabelle ein.

husband	detective	princess	dancer	king
uncle	lawyer	receptionist	widow	girlfriend
wife	granddaughter	niece	reporter	artist
teacher	aunt	boyfriend	pilot	engineer
violinist	prince	manager	grandfather	grandson
grandmother	nephew	tourist	queen	mechanic

MEN	WOMEN	BOTH
uncle	*aunt*	*pilot*

Können Sie noch andere Wörter für Frauen und Männer den Listen hinzufügen?

Schooldays

Schulzeit

**Ordnen Sie die folgenden Wörter der entsprechenden Kategorie zu.
Können Sie noch andere Wörter den Listen hinzufügen?**

desk	good/bad at	mathematics	ruler	secondary school
dictionary	headmistress	physics	take	schoolteacher
geography	lunch break	primary school	student	translate

SUBJECTS YOU LEARN	THINGS YOU USE

PLACES WHERE YOU LEARN	PEOPLE

VERBS	OTHER USEFUL WORDS AND PHRASES
. . . . an exam . . . . into English	

3. Kapitel

Topics
Themen

1. Werden Sie „Wortsammler"!

Manche Menschen sammeln Briefmarken, die sie in ihren Alben sortieren. Warum sollte man nicht auch **Wörter** sammeln?

2. Überlegen Sie gut, wo Sie Ihre gesammelten Wörter ablegen wollen.

Dieses Kapitel wird Ihnen helfen, Wörter nach verschiedenen Themenbereichen, z. B. Ferien, Zahlen, einzuordnen.

3. Zeichnen Sie Ihren eigenen Wortbaum.

Schauen Sie sich den Wortbaum auf Seite 25 an. Alle dort eingetragenen Begriffe ranken sich um ein bestimmtes Thema wie Äste und Blätter an einem Baum. Auf diese Weise lassen sich die Begriffe leichter einprägen.

4. Benutzen Sie Bilder.

Schauen Sie sich die Übung auf Seite 30 an. Manche Wörterbücher benutzen Bilder zur Erklärung von Begriffen. Schneiden Sie Bilder aus und kleben Sie sie in Ihr Vokabelheft. Tragen Sie dann die Wörter in die Bilder ein.

3.1 Numbers
Zahlen

Aufgabe 1

Schreiben Sie die folgenden Zahlen vor das entsprechende Wort.

0   1.5   2½   11   12   14   17   18   19   21   32   43   54
65   76   87   98   100   212   1,000   3,679   1,300,010

1. . . . . nineteen		11. . . . . one point five
2. . . . . . . eighteen		12. . . . . seventeen
3. . . . . . . eighty-seven		13. . . . . seventy-six
4. . . . . . . eleven		14. . . . . sixty-five
5. . . . . . . fifty-four		15. . . . . thirty-two
6. . . . . . . forty-three		16. . . . . a thousand
7. . . . . . . fourteen		17. . . . . twenty-one
8. . . . . . . a (one) hundred		18. . . . . two and a half
9. . . . . . . a dozen		19. . . . . two hundred and twelve
10. . . . . . . ninety-eight		20. . . . . zero

21. . . . . three thousand, six hundred and seventy-nine

22. . . . . one million, three hundred thousand and ten

Verdecken Sie jetzt die Wörter und sprechen Sie die Zahlen laut.

Aufgabe 2

Schreiben Sie die folgenden Wörter neben die entsprechende Zahl.

eighth   first   second   thirty-first   twenty-seventh   fifteenth   fourth
third   twelfth   twenty-third   fifth   ninth   thirtieth   twentieth

1. 1st		8. . . . . .12th
2. 2nd		9. . . . . .15th
3. 3rd		10. . . . . .20th
4. 4th		11. . . . . .23rd
5. 5th		12. . . . . .27th
6. 8th		13. . . . . .30th
7. 9th		14. . . . . .31st

20

3.2 Dates
Daten

Aufgabe 1

Beachten Sie, wie Jahreszahlen im Englischen ausgesprochen werden:

1601	1999	2,000
sixteen oh one	nineteen ninety nine	the year two thousand

Ordnen Sie zunächst die Jahreszahlen den Ereignissen zu. Schreiben Sie dann die Jahreszahlen aus.

a. 1789 b. 1989 c. 1945 d. 1969

1. The first man on the moon _____ . . . .

2. The start of the French Revolution _____ . . . .

3. The end of the 2nd World War _____ . . . .

4. The end of the Berlin Wall _____ . . . .

5. The next Olympic Games _____ . . . .

Aufgabe 2

Beachten Sie, wie Daten im Englischen ausgesprochen werden:

13th Nov = the thirteenth of November

May 17th = May the seventeenth

Wie sagt man folgende Daten?

1. 1st Jan. (New Year's Day) . . . .

2. Feb. 29th (Every 4 years!) . . . .

3. 4th July (US Independence Day) . . . .

4. Dec. 24th (Christmas Eve) . . . .

5. Your birthday . . . .

6. A national holiday in your country . . . .

7. A special date for you . . . .

Übrigens: May 17th heißt in Amerika auch: May seventeenth.

3.3 Time
Uhrzeit

You can say: three fifty   *or*   ten to four

      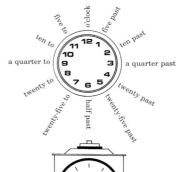

Schreiben Sie die Uhrzeit unter die Uhren.

1. . . . .   2. . . . .   3. . . . .

4. . . . .   5. . . . .   6. . . . .

7. . . . .   8. . . . .   9. . . . .

10. nearly . . . .   11. just after . . . . . .   12. almost . . . .

Beachten Sie: Bei Zug- und Flugverbindungen sagt man häufig:

13.50	thirteen fifty	16.30	sixteen thirty
12.00	twelve noon	19.00	nineteen hundred hours

Places and prepositions
Orte und Präpositionen

Aufgabe 1

Ordnen Sie die Satzhälften auf der rechten Seite der passenden Hälfte auf der linken Seite zu. Tragen Sie Ihre Antwort in die darunterstehenden Kästchen ein.

1.	You can park your car	a.	at university.
2.	You can study engineering	b.	from this office.
3.	You can catch the fast train	c.	on the radio.
4.	You can have a room	d.	in the first floor restaurant.
5.	You can get to work	f.	in the space next to mine.
6.	You can have breakfast	g.	on the fourth floor.
7.	You can send a fax	h.	from the central station.
8.	You can listen to the news	i.	on the bus.

1.		2.		3.		4.		5.		6.		7.		8.	

Aufgabe 2

Fügen Sie nun auch diese Sätze zusammen.

1.	You can improve your vocabulary	a.	out in the country.
2.	You can visit my aunt	b.	in the gym if you book it.
3.	You can live more cheaply	c.	at her flat in Washington.
4.	You can play basketball	d.	at the optician's in an hour.
5.	You can drive to work	f.	at the traffic lights.
6.	You can get new lenses	g.	in my car if you want.
7.	You can cross	h.	at the party!
8.	You can't wear that dress	i.	on your own or in class.

1.		2.		3.		4.		5.		6.		7.		8.	

Tragen Sie das jeweils beste Wort in die Sätze ein.

1. Margaret is my best . . . . I tell her everything.
   a. woman   b. friend   c. pet   d. enemy

2. Excuse me. Can you tell me the way to the town hall?
   I'm afraid not. I'm a . . . . around here.
   a. conductor   b. foreigner   c. tourist   d. stranger

3. They invited over 50 . . . . to their daughter's wedding.
   a. guests   b. hosts   c. nieces   d. priests

4. Excuse me, sir. Are you the . . . . of this car?
   a. stranger   b. owner   c. pilot   d. rider

5. Louise is a . . . . in our National Orchestra.
   a. piano   b. florist   c. violin   d. violinist

6. The . . . . at the garage said my car needed a new engine.
   a. athlete   b. mechanic   c. officer   d. engineer

7. Good morning, ... I'm the manager. How can I help you?
   a. boy   b. man   c. mister   d. sir

8. Michelle is a . . . . so it's difficult for her to understand what
   people say if they speak very fast.
   a. beginner   b. customer   c. starter   d. winner

9. Trevor works as a shop . . . . in a big store.
   a. assistant   b. attendant   c. brother   d. instructor

10. My . . . . was never happy about me marrying her daughter.
    a. mother-in-law b. uncle   c. nephew   d. stepfather

11. Joe's doctor wasn't sure what was wrong with him so she sent him to
    a . . . . at the hospital.
    a. principal   b. specialist   c. manager   d. writer

12. The steward served coffee to the first-class . . . .
    a. assistants   b. attendants   c. passengers   d. pilots

13. That . . . . wants to write about you in his newspaper.
    a. coach   b. cook   c. journalist   d. professor

14. A . . . . looks after our children when we go out for the evening.
    a. babysitter   b. butcher   c. cleaner   d. disc jockey

3.6 Hobbies
Hobbys

Eine gute Möglichkeit, Wörter einem bestimmten Thema zuzuordnen, ist die hier abgebildete Zeichnung. Wie Sie sehen, sind hier nur einige der möglichen Begriffe eingetragen. Welche anderen Wörter fallen Ihnen noch ein?

Tragen Sie diese Wörter in die Zeichnung ein.

camera	horror	referee	take	cowboy	lose
shorts	video	guitar	penalty	stadium	violin

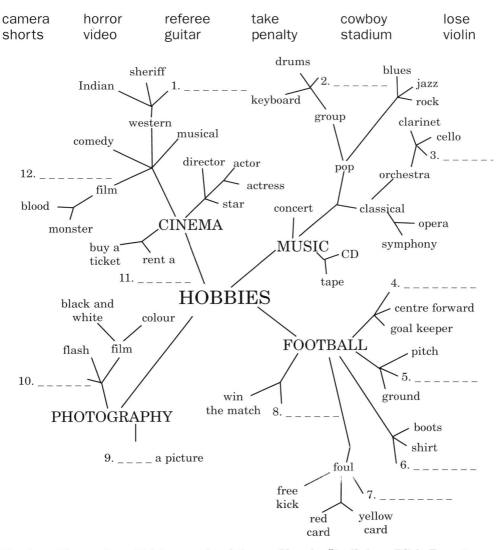

Denken Sie an Ihre Hobbys und zeichnen Sie ein ähnliches Bild. Benutzen Sie dazu ein großes Blatt Papier!

Tragen Sie die Wörter in die Zeichnung ein.

airport	caravan	guide book	restaurant	swimming
aspirin	credit card	pool	single room	train
bike	disco	receptionist	suitcase	yacht

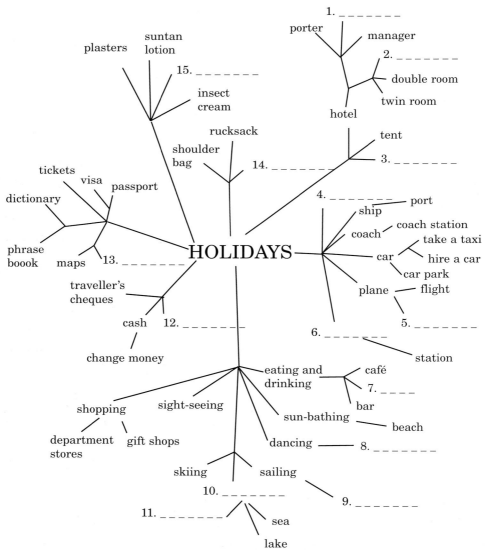

Fallen Ihnen noch mehr Wörter für diese Zeichnung ein?

3.8 Jobs
Berufe

Ordnen Sie die Berufsbezeichnungen den entsprechenden Bildern zu.

car mechanic	footballer	nurse	priest	teacher
tourist guide	hairdresser	office worker	sailor	cook
shop assistant	librarian	pilot	doctor	waiter
factory worker	lorry driver	plumber	taxi driver	vet

1. . . . . 2. . . . . 3. . . . . 4. . . . .

5. . . . . 6. . . . . 7. . . . . 8. . . . .

9. . . . . 10. . . . . 11. . . . . 12. . . . .

13. . . . . 14. . . . . 15. . . . . 16. . . . .

17. . . . . 18. . . . . 19. . . . . 20. . . . .

Schreiben Sie die Sätze unter das entsprechende Bild.

We hired a car.	We came on our bikes.	We came on foot.
We came by train.	We got the car ferry.	We took the underground.
We flew.	We took a taxi.	We went by bus.

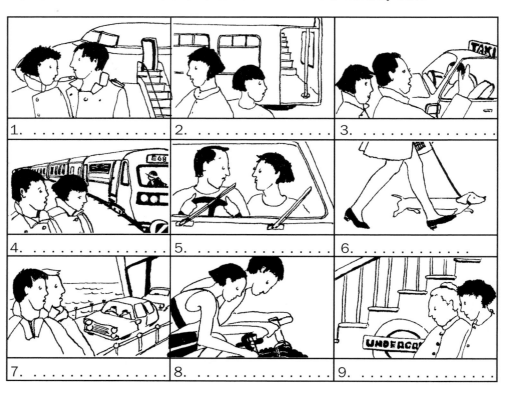

1. . . . .
2. . . . .
3. . . . .

4. . . . .
5. . . . .
6. . . . .

7. . . . .
8. . . . .
9. . . . .

Tragen Sie nun die richtigen Wörter in die Sätze ein.

coaches	walk	cycle	by boat	by plane

1. If you fly, you go . . . .

2. Buses for long journeys are usually called . . . .

3. If you go on a ferry, you can also say . . . .

4. If you go on foot, you. . . . .

5. If you go by bike, you . . . .

Schreiben Sie die Sätze unter das entsprechende Bild.

We kissed goodnight.	I was busy all afternoon.	I went to the dentist.
I got up at 7.30.	I had a meeting at 9.	I met Mark for lunch.
I had a shower.	We had dinner.	I waited for the bus.

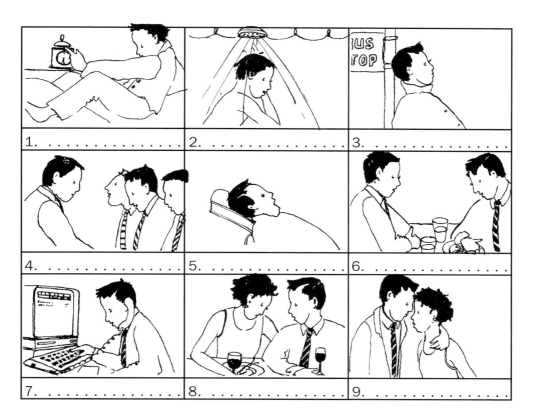

1. ....
2. ....
3. ....
4. ....
5. ....
6. ....
7. ....
8. ....
9. ....

Welche Wörter kommen in den Bildern nach „have"?

have a s _ _ _ _ _   have a _ _ _ _ _ _ g   have _ _ _ _ e_

Welche acht Begriffe können auf „have" folgen?

a sandwich	a headache	cold	a good time	a coffee
a problem	hunger	an idea	a bad throat	a beer

In the street
Auf der Straße

Schreiben Sie die Wörter unter das entsprechende Bild.

road sign	lamp post	motorbike	pram	phone box
bus stop	litter bin	pavement	bike	traffic lights
crossing	lorry	policeman	van	public toilet (loo)

1. . . . .

2. . . . .

3. . . . .

4. . . . .

5. . . . .

6. . . . .

7. . . . .

8. . . . .

9. . . . .

10. . . . .

11. . . . .

12. . . . .

13. . . . .

14. . . . .

15. . . . .

Common things (1)

Dinge des Alltags (1)

Schreiben Sie die Wörter unter das entsprechende Bild.

comb	pencil	credit card	wallet	envelope
key	glasses	calculator	coins	scissors
pen	stamp	magazine	notes	file
watch	clock	toothbrush	cheque	contact lenses

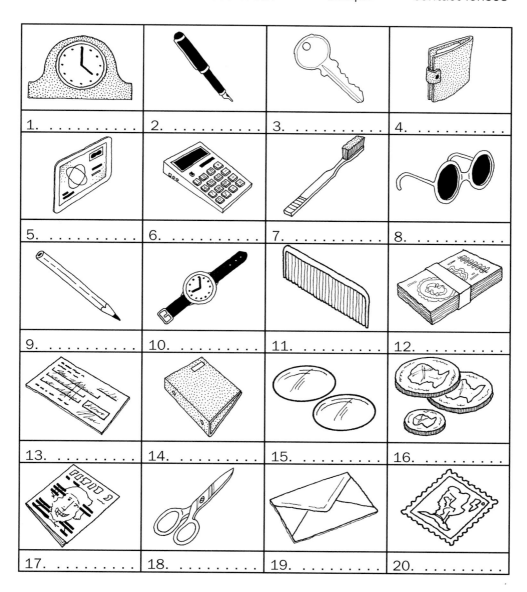

1. . . . .
2. . . . .
3. . . . .
4. . . . .

5. . . . .
6. . . . .
7. . . . .
8. . . . .

9. . . . .
10. . . . .
11. . . . .
12. . . . .

13. . . . .
14. . . . .
15. . . . .
16. . . . .

17. . . . .
18. . . . .
19. . . . .
20. . . . .

Common things (2)

Dinge des Alltags (2)

Schreiben Sie die Bezeichnungen unter das entsprechende Bild.

camera	personal CD	radio/cassette recorder
camcorder	stereo system	personal stereo
car stereo	headphones	mobile phone

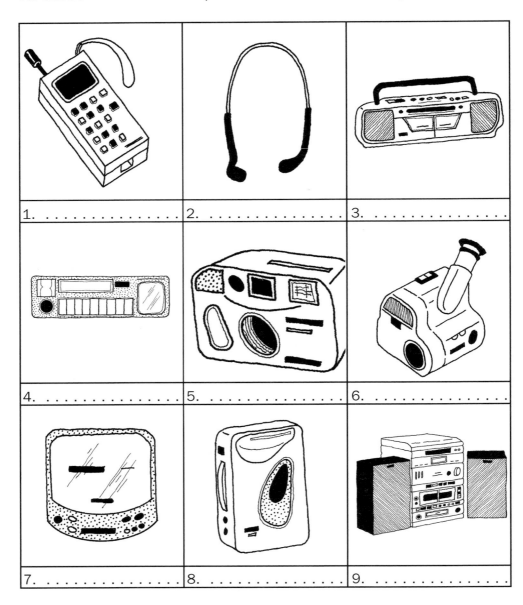

1. . . . .

2. . . . .

3. . . . .

4. . . . .

5. . . . .

6. . . . .

7. . . . .

8. . . . .

9. . . . .

Fruit and vegetables
Obst und Gemüse

Schreiben Sie die folgenden Wörter unter das entsprechende Bild.

apple	beans	banana	lettuce	cucumber	onions
peas	peach	cabbage	orange	potatoes	lemon
pear	grapes	carrot	cherries	tomatoes	pineapple

FRUIT

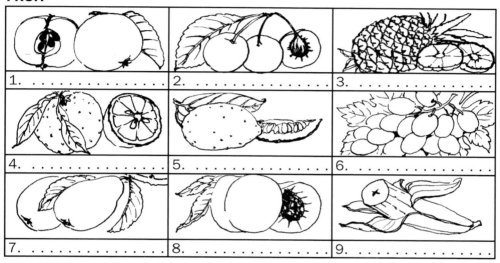

1. . . . .
2. . . . .
3. . . . .

4. . . . .
5. . . . .
6. . . . .

7. . . . .
8. . . . .
9. . . . .

VEGETABLES

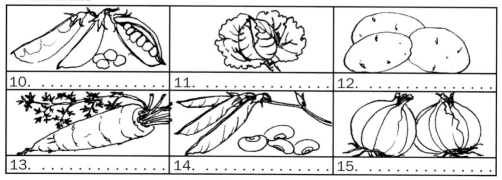

10. . . . .
11. . . . .
12. . . . .

13. . . . .
14. . . . .
15. . . . .

SALAD

16. . . . .
17. . . . .
18. . . . .

Sports
Sport

Schreiben Sie die folgenden Sportarten unter das entsprechende Bild.

cycling	golf	sailing	basketball	American football
fishing	skiing	skating	swimming	riding
football	tennis	surfing	windsurfing	table tennis

1. . . . .

2. . . . .

3. . . . .

4. . . . .

5. . . . .

6. . . . .

7. . . . .

8. . . . .

9. . . . .

10. . . . .

11. . . . .

12. . . . .

13. . . . .

14. . . . .

15. . . . .

3.16 Clothes
Kleidung

Schreiben Sie die folgenden Wörter unter das entsprechende Bild.

anorak	coat	jacket	skirt	T-shirt	jumper/sweater/pullover
boots	dress	scarf	trainers	tights	knickers/pants
bra	shirt	shoe	socks	trousers	track-suit
cap	hat	shorts	suit	underpants	jeans

1. . . . .
2. . . . .
3. . . . .
4. . . . .

5. . . . .
6. . . . .
7. . . . .
8. . . . .

9. . . . .
10. . . . .
11. . . . .
12. . . . .

13. . . . .
14. . . . .
15. . . . .
16. . . . .

17. . . . .
18. . . . .
19. . . . .
20. . . . .

21. . . . .
22. . . . .
23. . . . .
24. . . . .

3.17 Restaurant food
Im Restaurant

Dies ist eine Liste von Dingen, die man auf einer Speisekarte im Restaurant finden kann. Tragen Sie die Wörter an die entsprechende Stelle auf der Speisekarte ein.

ice cream	vegetable soup	roast pork	peas
lobster	apple pie	sole	yoghurt
chocolate mousse	rump steak	fruit juice	beans
roast potatoes	cauliflower	baked potato	carrots
lamb cutlets	Scottish salmon	mashed potato	fruit salad
grilled trout	roast chicken	French fries	

STARTERS

. . . .

MAIN COURSES

FISH/SHELLFISH	MEAT	VEGETABLES	POTATOES
. . . .	. . . .	. . . .	. . . .
. . . .	. . . .	. . . .	. . . .
. . . .	. . . .	. . . .	. . . .
. . . .	. . . .	. . . .	. . . .

DESSERTS

. . . .

. . . .

Wenn Sie diese Übung beendet haben, sollte noch Platz für ein Dessert sein. Welches ist Ihr Lieblingsdessert? Schlagen Sie den englischen Begriff dafür nach und tragen Sie es an dieser Stelle ein.

4. Kapitel

Word Formation
Wortbildung

1. Aus Wörtern kann man Wörter machen.

Viele Wörter gehören zu miteinander verwandten Familien, zum Beispiel:

You study	>	<u>science</u>
The person	>	<u>a scientist</u>
The adjective	>	<u>scientific</u>

2. Versuchen Sie, Wörter zu bilden.

Wenn Sie ein neues Wort lernen, schlagen Sie in Ihrem Wörterbuch dessen „Verwandte" nach. Tragen Sie auch diese in Ihr Vokabelheft ein.

3. Bilden Sie Wortfamilien.

Sie werden eine Menge neuer Wörter lernen, indem Sie Wörter innerhalb ihrer Familien studieren. Dadurch können Sie ebenso lernen, wie sich neue Wörter bilden lassen.

4.1 **Making adjectives**
Adjektivbildung

Vervollständigen Sie die Sätze mit einer Form des Wortes in Klammern. Beispiel:

It's too . *windy* . . . . to wear a hat today. (WIND)

Die neuen Wörter enden auf *-ed*, *-ful*, *-ing*, oder *-y*.

1. Be . . . . ! You might break something! (CARE)

2. If it's . . . . tomorrow, let's go to the beach. (SUN)

3. Lenny looked very . . . . when he saw us. (SURPRISE)

4. We've got some very . . . . news for you. (SURPRISE)

5. We watched a very . . . . show on television last night. (FUN)

6. Mum gets . . . . when Jill is so late. (WORRY)

7. In . . . . weather like this the yachts usually stay in the harbour. (STORM)

8. In my country most . . . . men don't wear a ring. (MARRY)

9. I went to an . . . . talk about finding a job. (INTEREST)

10. Bye! Have a . . . . holiday! (WONDER)

11. Sheila lives in a very . . . . part of the country. (BEAUTY)

12. John usually feels . . . . after a big meal. (SLEEP)

13. A calculator can be very . . . . if you work in a shop. (USE)

14. Gina was very . . . . when people stared at her new hairdo. (EMBARRASS)

15. It's really . . . . sitting at a computer all day. (TIRE)

16. As the plane came nearer the airport, we all got very . . . . (EXCITE)

Making nouns
Nomenbildung

Vervollständigen Sie die Sätze mit einer Form des Wortes in Klammern. Beispiel:

I've got an *invitation* . to a party tonight.   (INVITE)

Die neuen Wörter enden auf *-er, -ing,* oder *-tion.*

1. We have an electric . . . . in our kitchen but my mother has gas.   (COOK)

2. My office is in a big . . . . near the bus station.   (BUILD)

3. Have you got any . . . . about flights to Los Angeles?   (INFORM)

4. What's the . . . . of the word "exhausted" ?   (MEAN)

5. Can you help me? I don't understand how this video . . . . works.   (RECORD)

6. The . . . . of the book is good but it gets boring.   (BEGIN)

7. I'm going to town to do some . . . . Do you want to come with me?   (SHOP)

8. We went to an interesting . . . . of old cars at a large house in the country.   (EXHIBIT)

9. Have you got a . . . . I can put my jacket on?   (HANG)

10. I'm afraid . . . . is not permitted in this room.   (SMOKE)

11. We made this ice cream with our own ice-cream . . . .   (MAKE)

12. Stop! Come back! You're going in the wrong . . . . !   (DIRECT)

13. What time does the . . . . start this evening?   (MEET)

14. Juan bought a Spanish . . . . of Animal Farm.   (TRANSLATE)

15. Is there any ice cream in the . . . . ?   (FREEZE)

16. Now we have central . . . . , the house is much warmer.   (HEAT)

17. Sarah has over ten thousand stamps in her . . . .   (COLLECT)

18. There's a . . . . of a horse on the wall by Mary's bed.   (PAINT)

4.3 Nouns for people
Nomen für Menschen

Wenn Sie ein Wort in Ihrem Wörterbuch nachschlagen, überprüfen Sie auch, ob sich daraus andere Wörter bilden lassen. Beispiel:

farm ➔ farmer, visit ➔ visitor

Schreiben Sie die Bezeichnungen für die Personen neben folgende Wörter. Die neuen Wörter enden auf -er oder -or.

1. act . . . .
2. bake . . . .
3. collect . . . .
4. direct . . . .
5. drive . . . .
6. farm . . . .
7. garden . . . .
8. inspect . . . .
9. instruct . . . .
10. manage . . . .

11. operate . . . .
12. play . . . .
13. report . . . .
14. ride . . . .
15. run . . . .
16. sail . . . .
17. teach . . . .
18. translate . . . .
19. visit . . . .
20. work . . . .

Benutzen Sie nun einige dieser Nomen zur Vervollständigung folgender Sätze.

1. Are you sure this taxi . . . . knows where he's going?

2. My bank . . . . doesn't want to lend me any more money.

3. I'm a stamp . . . . in my spare time.

4. A newspaper . . . . wants to ask you about your accident.

5. A good football . . . . can make a lot of money.

6. I think my driving . . . . was surprised when I passed my test.

4.4 Countries – nationalities
Länder – Nationalitäten

In dieser Übung sehen Sie vier Listen von Ländern und Nationalitäten. Tragen Sie die folgenden Wörter an der entsprechenden Stelle ein.

Brazilian	Canada	Chinese	Finnish	French	German
Greece	Hungary	Ireland	Japan	Lebanese	Mexican
Omani	Polish	Portugal	Russia	Scotland	Spanish
Switzerland	Taiwanese	Thai	Turkey	Vietnam	Wales

-an		**-ish**	
Brazil	*Brazilian* . . .	Finland	*Finnish* . . .
. . . .	Canadian	. . . .	Irish
Germany	. . . .	Poland	. . . .
. . . .	Hungarian	. . . .	Scottish
Mexico	. . . .	Spain	. . . .
. . . .	Russian	. . . .	Turkish
. . . .		. . . .	
. . . .		. . . .	
. . . .		. . . .	

-ese		**others**	
China	. . . .	France	. . . .
. . . .	Japanese	. . . .	Greek
Lebanon	. . . .	Oman	. . . .
. . . .	Portuguese	. . . .	Swiss
Taiwan	. . . .	Thailand	. . . .
. . . .	Vietnamese	. . . .	Welsh
. . . .		. . . .	
. . . .		. . . .	
. . . .		. . . .	

Befindet sich Ihr Heimatland in einer der Listen? Falls nicht, tragen Sie es an der entsprechenden Stelle ein. Tragen Sie auch andere Länder und Nationalitäten, die Sie kennen, ein.

Für diese Übung benötigen Sie vielleicht Ihr Wörterbuch. Schlagen Sie die in Großbuchstaben geschriebenen Wörter nach. Dort sollten Sie auch ein Wort aus der gleichen Familie finden, mit dem Sie dann die Sätze vervollständigen können.

1. FLY
   I want to be a pilot. I'm having . . . . lessons. **adjective**

2. DAY
   Is the Times the best . . . . newspaper? **adjective**

3. ILL
   Sam's got a very serious . . . . **noun**

4. ANGRY
   Pat's . . . . didn't go away. It got worse! **noun**

5. COMPOSE
   Some people think Mozart was the greatest . . . . **noun**

6. FAULT
   My new radio is . . . . **adjective**

7. POLITICS
   Greg's a left-wing . . . . **noun**

8. STORM
   It was very . . . . last night. **adjective**

9. POSSIBLE
   There are lots of . . . . **noun**

10. SHORT
    They want to . . . . our lunch break! **verb**

11. HEALTH
    A . . . . mind in a . . . . body. **adjective**

12. HEAR
    Sue's . . . . was damaged when the bomb went off. **noun**

5. Kapitel

Spelling and Pronunciation
Rechtschreibung und Aussprache

1. Ein Wort ist mehr als nur seine Bedeutung.

Wenn Sie ein neues Wort lernen, lernen Sie seine Bedeutung und vielleicht übersetzen Sie es auch in Ihre Sprache. Prägen Sie sich gleichzeitig aber auch seine Aussprache und Schreibweise ein.

2. Phonetische Symbole

In allen guten Wörterbüchern finden Sie hinter jedem Eintrag die Aussprache in Lautschrift angegeben, zum Beispiel:

phonetics [fənetɪks].

Wenn Sie die Symbole lesen können, wird Ihnen das Lernen der Aussprache neuer Wörter problemlos gelingen.

Vowel sounds

Vokalaussprache

Im Englischen ist es manchmal recht schwierig, die Aussprache oder die Schreibweise eines Wortes zu erraten. Deshalb ist es wichtig, die phonetische Lautschrift, die in Ihrem Wörterbuch verwendet wird, zu lernen.
Mit ihrer Hilfe können Sie die Aussprache neuer Wörter erkennen. In der folgenden Aufgabe werden Sie einige der Symbole üben und feststellen, welche unterschiedlichen Schreibweisen sie haben.

Tragen Sie diese Wörter entsprechend der Aussprache ihrer Vokale in eine der Listen ein.

boot	here	new	steak	toe	wear
chair	know	phone	their	top	what
cheer	make	rain	they	two	where
dear	near	shop	toast	want	you

1. [ɒ]
(lot)

. . . .

. . . .

. . . .

. . . .

2. [uː]
(too)

. . . .

. . . .

. . . .

. . . .

3. [eə]
(there)

. . . .

. . . .

. . . .

. . . .

4. [eɪ]
(say)

. . . .

. . . .

. . . .

. . . .

5. [ɪə]
(ear)

. . . .

. . . .

. . . .

. . . .

6. [əʊ]
(go)

. . . .

. . . .

. . . .

. . . .

Same sound (1)

Gleiche Aussprache (1)

Im Englischen gibt es Wörter, die zwar die gleiche Aussprache, aber eine unterschiedliche Schreibweise und Bedeutung haben, zum Beispiel:

it's   its   there   they're   their

Es ist sinnvoll, eine Liste aller Ihnen bekannten Wörter mit gleicher Aussprache anzulegen. Damit können Sie jederzeit überprüfen, ob Sie die richtige Schreibweise verwendet haben.

Benutzen Sie jeweils eines der Wortpaare, um die Sätze zu vervollständigen.

buy/by	it's/its	sea/see	too/two
hear/here	right/write	son/sun	who's/whose

1. a. I like swimming and my friend does, ...

    b. Anne has . . . . children, a girl and a boy.

2. a. My . . . ., Bob, works in a car factory.

    b. When the . . . . shines, everyone feels much better.

3. a. They live by the . . . . and often go sailing.

    b. It's too dark in here! I can't . . . . anything!

4. a. Oh dear! I think . . . . raining!

    b. The plant I bought lost all . . . . leaves.

5. a. I'm going to the shops to . . . . a birthday card.

    b. Could you sit over there, ... the window?

6. a. Don't speak so softly. I can't . . . . you.

    b. Henry, come . . . . a moment, please.

7. a. My house is the third one on the . . . .

    b. If you want to come, please . . . . your name on the list.

8. a. I have a friend . . . . studying at university.

    b. I have a friend . . . . father is a journalist.

Same sound (2)
Gleiche Aussprache (2)

Benutzen Sie jeweils eines der Wortpaare, um die Sätze zu vervollständigen.

fair/fare	meat/meet	some/sum	wait/weight
hour/our	pair/pear	their/there	weak/week
knew/new	passed/past	there/they're	wood/would

1. a. We . . . . the sports club on our way home.

   b. We went . . . . the sports club on our way home.

2. a. I thought I . . . . the answer but I was wrong.

   b. What do you think of Neil's . . . . motorbike?

3. a. The students are worried about . . . . exams.

   b. Why aren't . . . . more plays on television?

4. a. You should work for an . . . . and then take a break.

   b. We're very pleased with . . . . new video.

5. a. This chair is made of . . . ., not plastic.

   b. Milly . . . . really like to go out with Paul.

6. a. She's a vegetarian. She doesn't eat . . . .

   b. Shall we . . . . outside the cinema at half past?

7. a. I have a terrible headache and feel very . . . .

   b. Only one more . . . . and then it's my holiday!

8. a. We need . . . . more butter.

   b. Can you do this . . . . ? I'm hopeless at maths!

9. a. Could you put the bags over . . . . in the corner?

   b. Who are those people? < I think . . . . tourists.

10. a. He's quite tall and has . . . . hair.

    b. How much is the cheapest . . . . to New York?

11. a. I'd like to buy a . . . . of trousers.

    b. Which would you prefer – a . . . . or a banana?

12. a. I usually . . . . for the bus near the town hall.

    b. What's the . . . . of your luggage? < 20 kilos.

Rhymes
Reime

Die folgenden Listen enthalten vier Wörter, von denen sich jeweils drei reimen. Suchen Sie das Wort, das nicht in die Liste paßt und kreisen Sie es ein.

1. call	fall	(shall)	wall
2. clown	down	own	town
3. feel	meal	she'll	well
4. above	glove	love	move
5. cow	go	know	throw
6. gun	one	phone	sun
7. bought	caught	coat	sort
8. clear	dear	hear	pear
9. hair	here	there	wear
10. cost	most	post	roast
11. after	daughter	quarter	shorter
12. eat	great	hate	wait
13. boot	route	shoot	shout
14. my	pie	tea	tie
15. do	new	no	through
16. arm	calm	farm	warm
17. laid	paid	said	stayed
18. great	late	wait	white

Stress patterns

Betonungsmuster

Tragen Sie die Wörter entsprechend ihrer Betonungsmuster in die Listen ein. Das ▼ Zeichen steht für die Silbe mit der Hauptbetonung, zum Beispiel:

▼ ○	○ ▼	▼ ○ ○	○ ▼ ○
music	arrive	photograph	mechanic

again	breakfast	enjoy	Japan
another	certainly	example	manager
April	December	holiday	musician
banana	difficult	hospital	sweater
begin	easy	hotel	telephone
between	eleven	husband	traffic

1. ▼ ○

. . . .

. . . .

. . . .

. . . .

. . . .

. . . .

2. ○ ▼

. . . .

. . . .

. . . .

. . . .

. . . .

. . . .

3. ▼ ○ ○

. . . .

. . . .

. . . .

. . . .

. . . .

. . . .

4. ○ ▼ ○

. . . .

. . . .

. . . .

. . . .

. . . .

. . . .

6. Kapitel

Word Partnerships
Wortpartnerschaften

1. Wörter gehören auf eine ganz bestimmte Art zusammen.

Normalerweise sagen wir im Englischen:

> I made a mistake.

Wir sagen nicht:

> I did a mistake.

Bei dem Wort *mistake* wird gewöhnlich *make* benutzt.
Make a mistake bezeichnen wir daher als „Wortpartnerschaft".

2. Wenn Sie ein Wort lernen, lernen Sie gleichzeitig die Wörter, die dazugehören.

Dies ist sehr wichtig. Einzelne Wörter werden nur selten isoliert benutzt. Sie verbessern Ihre Englischkenntnisse enorm, wenn Sie Wörter zusammen mit ihren „Partnern" lernen.

6.1 Verb + noun
Verb + Nomen

 Es ist wichtig, beim Wortschatzlernen darauf zu achten, welche Wörter zusammen auftreten. Es ist sinnvoller, beispielsweise eine Verb-Nomen Partnerschaft zu lernen, als das Nomen allein.

Aufgabe 1

Ordnen Sie den Verben auf der linken Seite ein Nomen der rechten Seite zu. Tragen Sie Ihre Antworten in die Kästchen ein.

1. do	a. the bell	1.	
2. listen to	b. a flat	2.	
3. post	c. hands	3.	
4. rent	d. your homework	4.	
5. ring	e. a letter	5.	
6. shake	f. the radio	6.	
7. tell	g. television	7.	
8. watch	h. the truth	8.	

Aufgabe 2

Und noch einmal: Ordnen Sie zu.

1. brush	a. a bus	1.	
2. catch	b. cards	2.	
3. change	c. the door	3.	
4. cross	d. your English	4.	
5. improve	e. your hair	5.	
6. lock	f. glasses	6.	
7. play	g. your mind	7.	
8. wear	h. the road	8.	

Benutzen Sie nun einige der Ausdrücke, um diese Sätze zu vervollständigen.

1. We usually . . . . when we meet people for the first time.
2. Jill has to . . . . because she can't see very well.
3. Have you got a stamp? I want to . . . . to my parents.
4. Building your vocabulary is the best way to . . . .

Aufgabe 1

Ordnen Sie die Adjektive auf der linken Seite einem Nomen der rechten Seite zu. Achtung! Obwohl einige Adjektive zu mehreren Hauptwörtern passen, sollten Sie jedes Wort nur einmal benutzen. Tragen Sie Ihre Antworten in die Kästchen ein.

1. comfortable		a. chair		1.	
2. dark		b. disco		2.	
3. empty		c. game		3.	
4. exciting		d. glass		4.	
5. heavy		e. hair		5.	
6. long		f. man		6.	
7. noisy		g. suitcase		7.	
8. single		h. time		8.	

Aufgabe 2

Tun Sie das Gleiche mit diesen Wörtern.

1. blonde		a. day		1.	
2. careful		b. driver		2.	
3. delicious		c. hair		3.	
4. interesting		d. lesson		4.	
5. loud		e. meal		5.	
6. married		f. mistake		6.	
7. silly		g. noise		7.	
8. sunny		h. woman		8.	

Benutzen Sie nun einige der Ausdrücke, um diese Sätze zu vervollständigen.

1. On a . . . . like this I usually go for a swim in the sea.
2. That isn't a very . . . . ! Why don't you sit here?
3. Sometimes you have to wait a . . . . before the bus comes.
4. I knew the answer, but I still made a . . . .

6.3 Useful verbs (1)
Nützliche Verben (1)

Aufgabe 1

Ordnen Sie die Verben unter den Bildern zu.

dance	miss	read	throw
drink	open	ride	walk
eat	paint	smile	write

1. . . . .
2. . . . .
3. . . . .
4. . . . .
5. . . . .
6. . . . .
7. . . . .
8. . . . .
9. . . . .
10. . . . .
11. . . . .
12. . . . .

Aufgabe 2

Setzen Sie Verben aus der obigen Liste sinnvoll ein.

1. . . . . the door

2. . . . . a picture

3. . . . . a pizza

4. . . . . the paper

5. . . . . a ball

6. . . . . a bike

7. . . . . a letter

8. . . . . the bus

Useful verbs (2)

Nützliche Verben (2)

Aufgabe 1

Ordnen Sie die Verben unter den Bildern zu.

climb	cut	fall	run
close	draw	jump	sing
cry	drive	kick	wash

1. . . . .
2. . . . .
3. . . . .
4. . . . .
5. . . . .
6. . . . .
7. . . . .
8. . . . .
9. . . . .
10. . . . .
11. . . . .
12. . . . .

Aufgabe 2

Setzen Sie Verben aus der obigen Liste sinnvoll ein.

1. . . . . your face
2. . . . . a song
3. . . . . a car
4. . . . . a picture

5. . . . . a football
6. . . . . a mountain
7. . . . . your nails
8. . . . . the door

6.5   Have, make, take
Have, make, take

Auf einige Verben können verschiedene Nomen folgen. Fallen Ihnen Nomen ein, die nach *have*, *make* und *take* kommen können? Machen Sie die folgende Übung und versuchen Sie, weitere Beispiele zu finden. Benutzen Sie die folgenden Worte jeweils nur einmal zur Vervollständigung der Sätze.

cake	cold	idea	picture	shower
call	difficulty	mistake	rest	taxi
care	friends	noise	seat	time

1. Can I use some of your shampoo? I'm going to have a . . . . and wash my hair.

2. You look tired. Why don't you lie down and have a . . . . ?

3. Lilian has a bad . . . . She can't stop sneezing.

4. I have an . . . . Why don't we have a party?

5. Mrs Fenton speaks so softly that we sometimes have . . . . hearing what she's saying.

6. I made a terrible . . . . ! I said 'got' was the past of 'go'!

7. Don't make so much . . . . ! I've got a headache.

8. Let's make Dave a chocolate . . . . for his birthday.

9. People are so nice in this village. It's easy to make . . . .

10. I want to make a . . . . to the United States but somebody's still using the phone.

11. There's no hurry. Take your . . . .

12. Come in, Mr Johnson. Please take a . . . .

13. Tony wanted to take a . . . . of the castle but he didn't have enough film.

14. Gill didn't walk to town. She took a . . . .

15. Take . . . . when you cross the main road. We don't want another accident!

 Unterstreichen Sie das Verb und das Nomen. So können Sie sich die Wortpartnerschaft leichter einprägen.

Common adjectives

Häufig gebrauchte Adjektive

Ordnen Sie die Adjektive der jeweils korrekten Gruppe von Nomen zu.

beautiful	big	cold	funny	great
high	long	old	strong	thick

	flower		journey
	woman		hair
1.	music	2.	way
	weather		fingernails
	view		road

	weather		coffee
	drink		wind
3.	day	4.	muscles
	meat		personality
	shower		belief

	pullover		mountain
	book		prices
5.	soup	6.	quality
	fog		speed
	forest		street

	story		man
	person		garden
7.	hat	8.	difference
	noise		mistake
	ideas		toe

	age		painter
	friend		distance
9.	clothes	10.	time
	custom		pleasure
	joke		holiday

6.7 Two-word expressions

Ausdrücke aus zwei Wörtern

Manchmal lassen sich im Englischen zwei Wörter verbinden, um einen gängigen Ausdruck zu bilden, zum Beispiel:

swimming pool   car park   orange juice

 Achten Sie auf derartige Begriffe, und tragen Sie sie in Ihr Vokabelheft ein.

Bilden Sie eine Partnerschaft zwischen einem Wort der linken Seite und einem Wort auf der rechten Seite. Tragen Sie Ihre Antworten in die Kästchen ein.

1. ice	a. book	1.	
2. driving	b. card	2.	
3. summer	c. centre	3.	
4. writing	d. cream	4.	
5. weather	e. floor	5.	
6. identity	f. forecast	6.	
7. football	g. holiday	7.	
8. diamond	h. licence	8.	
9. shop	i. match	9.	
10. soap	j. paper	10.	
11. shopping	k. powder	11.	
12. cheque	l. recorder	12.	
13. cassette	m. ring	13.	
14. ground	n. ticket	14.	
15. theatre	o. window	15.	

Benutzen Sie nun einige der Ausdrücke, um diese Sätze zu vervollständigen.

1. Last July we went to Rome for our . . . .

2. What would you like – the . . . . or the fruit salad?

3. The . . . . is for rain and then snow in the evening.

4. We had a room on the . . . . so we didn't have to use the lift.

7. Kapitel

Situations
Situationen

1. Feststehende Begriffe sind wichtig bei Unterhaltungen.

Wortschatz besteht nicht bloß aus Wörtern. Feststehende Redewendungen können auch sehr wichtig sein, besonders bei Unterhaltungen. Hier einige Beispiele:

How are you?

Nice to meet you.

Excuse me . . . .

2. Versuchen Sie, immer ein freundliches Englisch zu sprechen.

Feststehende Begriffe bei Unterhaltungen sind ein wichtiges
Zeichen von Freundlichkeit und Höflichkeit. Wer in bestimmten
Situationen einen falschen Ausdruck benutzt, könnte grob und
unhöflich wirken.

7.1 Everyday situations
Alltagssituationen

Ordnen Sie diese Antworten den entsprechenden Sätzen in den Bildern zu.

She doesn't feel very well.
Certainly. Here you are.
Oh no! What shall we do?
Nothing special. Why?

Yes, I am. Can I help you?
Thank you. It's nice to be here.
Thank you. The same to you.
That's all right. It doesn't matter.

58

Ordnen Sie die Sätze auf der linken Seite den Orten auf der rechten Seite zu.

1. Three stamps for Russia, please.	a. in a hotel
2. A table for two, please.	b. in the newsagent's
3. I'd like my eyes tested, please.	c. at the hairdresser's
4. A day return to Oxford, please.	d. in the baker's
5. Six oranges, please.	e. in a restaurant
6. A bottle of aspirin, please.	f. at the station
7. A small brown loaf, please.	g. in the post office
8. Not too short at the back, please.	h. in the optician's
9. A single room with bath, please.	i. in the chemist's
10. The Sunday Times, please.	j. in the greengrocer's

Tragen Sie Ihre Antworten hier ein.

1.	2.	3.	4.	5.	6.	7.	8.	9.	10.

Was sagt man sonst noch an diesen Orten?

A single to Gatwick, please. . . . .

. . . .

. . . .

. . . .

. . . .

7.3 At a restaurant

Im Restaurant

1. Gespräch

Benutzen Sie die folgenden Ausdrücke zur Vervollständigung des ersten Teils des Gesprächs.

for me, too	I'd like	soup of the day
What would you like	Are you ready	

Waiter   (1) . . . . to order now?

Andy   Yes, I think so.   (2) . . . . to start with, Helen?

Helen   What's the (3) . . . . ?

Waiter   Vegetable, madam.

Helen   O.K. Vegetable soup for me, please.

Andy   And (4) . . . ., please.

Waiter   And for the main course, Madam?

Helen   (5) . . . . roast chicken with mashed potato and peas, please.

Andy   And I'll have spaghetti bolognese.

2. Gespräch

Tun Sie das Gleiche mit dem zweiten Teil des Gesprächs.

What a pity	Thank you very much	I'm very sorry
something to drink	How would you like it	

Waiter   (1) . . . . but I'm afraid we haven't got any left, sir.

Andy   Oh dear! (2) . . . . ! Then I'll have the rump steak.

Waiter   (3) . . . ., sir?

Andy   Medium, please.

Waiter   And which vegetables would you like with that, sir?

Andy   French fries and peas, please.

Waiter   Would you like (4) . . . . ?

Helen   A glass of red wine, please.

Andy   And a bottle of mineral water for me, please.

Waiter   (5) . . . .

Asking the way
Nach dem Weg fragen

1. Gespräch

Vervollständigen Sie das Gespräch mit folgenden Wörtern.

I'm afraid not	Pardon	Could you tell me the way
Good idea	Excuse me	Why don't you ask

Mike   (1) . . . .

Silvia   Yes?

Mike   (2) . . . . to the nearest post office,
           please?

Silvia   (3) . . . . ?

Mike   Do you know where the nearest post office is?

Silvia   No, (4) . . . . I'm a stranger around
           here. (5) . . . . that policeman over there?

Mike   Oh yes. (6) . . . . Thanks.

2. Gespräch

Tun Sie das Gleiche mit diesem Gespräch.

the second on the right	how to get to	You're welcome
just after a supermarket	turn left	of course

Mike   Excuse me. Could you tell me (1) . . . . the
           nearest post office, please?

PC Stone   Yes, (2) . . . . Go down this street and
           (3) . . . . , at the traffic lights. Take
           (4) . . . . That's the road with a cinema
           on the corner. The post office is about a hundred metres along
           the road on the right, (5) . . . .

Mike   So that's left at the traffic lights, then second right. Thanks
           very much.

PC Stone   (6) . . . .

7.5 At a party
Auf einer Party

Aufgabe 1

Dies sind einige kurze Gespräche auf einer Party. Ordnen Sie die Reaktionen a. bis h. den Sätzen 1. bis 8. zu. Tragen Sie Ihre Antworten in die Kästchen ein.

1. What do you do?
2. How far is that from here?
3. What nationality are you?
4. Hello! My name's Mike Smith.
5. What do you do in your spare time?
6. Where do you come from?
7. Where do you live?
8. How do you spell that?

a. In a flat in Baker Street.
b. I like taking photos.
c. Mexico.
d. T-H-O-M-S-O-N.
e. Pleased to meet you.
f. Austrian.
g. About 6 kilometres.
h. I'm a journalist.

1.	2.	3.	4.	5.	6.	7.	8.

Aufgabe 2

Tun Sie das Gleiche bei dieser Aufgabe.

1. What star sign are you?
2. How are you?
3. I'll have to go in a minute.
4. What's the time?
5. Have you got a light?
6. Hello, Sarah.
7. Thanks for inviting me.
8. What would you like to drink?

a. What? So soon?
b. About half past eleven.
c. Thanks for coming.
d. Just an orange juice, please.
e. Hi, Andy.
f. Fine thanks. And you?
g. Leo. What's yours?
h. No, I'm afraid not. I don't smoke.

1.	2.	3.	4.	5.	6.	7.	8.

8. Kapitel

Word Grammar
Wortgrammatik

1. **Grammatik besteht aus Wörtern und Regeln.**

   Mit Grammatik verbindet man gewöhnlich Zeiten und Regeln. Aber Grammatik hat auch viel mit Wörtern zu tun – z. B. Mehrzahlformen, Präpositionen, Nomen, Adjektive. Außerdem handelt sie von der Art und Weise, wie diese Wörter zusammenpassen. Verbessern Sie Ihr Englisch, indem Sie sich mit der Grammatik der Wörter beschäftigen.

2. **Schreiben Sie Ähnliches zusammen auf.**

   Tragen Sie wiederkehrende Muster gemeinsam in Ihr Vokabelheft ein, zum Beispiel:

   Adjektiv + Präposition

   Verb + *at*

   Verb + *to*

   Es ist von großem Nutzen, Grammatik auf diese Art zu betrachten.

8.1 Plurals

Mehrzahlformen

Die meisten Nomen bilden die Mehrzahl durch Anhängen von „s", z. B.:

book ➤ books, shoe ➤ shoes

Bei einigen Nomen ist das nicht ganz so einfach, z. B.:

dress ➤ dresses, family ➤ families

Es lohnt sich, bei neugelernten Nomen, auch die Mehrzahlform zu prüfen.

Aufgabe 1

Bilden Sie die Mehrzahl dieser Nomen.

1.	baby	. . . .	8.	knife	. . . .
2.	box	. . . .	9.	leaf	. . . .
3.	boy	. . . .	10.	lunch	. . . .
4.	child	. . . .	11.	man	. . . .
5.	class	. . . .	12.	tomato	. . . .
6.	day	. . . .	13.	tooth	. . . .
7.	factory	. . . .	14.	woman	. . . .

Aufgabe 2

Vervollständigen Sie diese Sätze mit der Mehrzahl des Nomens in Klammern.

1. More . . . . ? < No thanks. I really couldn't.   (STRAWBERRY)

2. Big . . . . make too much noise.   (LORRY)

3. All the . . . . except the 6B go to the town centre.   (BUS)

4. Let's take our . . . . to the park.   (SANDWICH)

5. Good evening, ... and . . . .   (LADY, GENTLEMAN)

6. My . . . . are really sore after all that walking.   (FOOT)

Fallen Ihnen noch weitere Nomen mit ungewöhnlichen Pluralformen ein?

8.2 Opposites – verbs
Gegensätze – Verben

Ordnen sie jedem Verb sein Gegenteil aus dem Kasten zu.

1. agree *disagree*   8. hate   . . . .
2. ask   . . . .   9. land   . . . .
3. borrow   . . . .   10. laugh   . . . .
4. close   . . . .   11. leave   . . . .
5. come down . . . .   12. remember   . . . .
6. find   . . . .   13. sell   . . . .
7. finish   . . . .   14. take off   . . . .

answer	lend
arrive	lose
buy	love
cry	open
disagree	put on
forget	start
go up	take off

Vervollständigen Sie diese Sätze nun mit den Wortpaaren. Benutzen Sie jedes Paar nur einmal.

15. We expect the party to . . *finish/start* . . . . . at about six.

16. Some shops . . . . at seven o'clock.

17. Why did you . . . . so much money?

18. I . . . . going to discos.

19. Where did you . . . . your watch? < In the restaurant.

20. The train should . . . . at five thirty.

21. Why can't you . . . . what she said?

22. How many postcards did you . . . . ?

23. James started to . . . . when he heard the news.

24. Does anybody else want to . . . . any questions?

25. I hope prices will . . . . soon.

26. Please . . . . that jacket. You look ridiculous.

27. What time does their plane . . . . ?

28. I . . . . with most of what Brian says.

Opposites – adjectives

Gegensätze – Adjektive

Vervollständigen Sie die Sätze mit dem Gegenteil des Wortes in Klammern. Benutzen Sie die folgenden Wörter jeweils ein Mal.

bad	difficult	late	open
big	fast	left	tall
cold	first	long	young
expensive	high	new	wrong

1. Now this question is very . . . . (EASY)

2. Be careful! The water is very . . . . ! (HOT)

3. I see you're wearing your . . . . jacket today. (OLD)

4. You're too . . . . to go to a disco. (OLD)

5. Food is . . . . in this country. (CHEAP)

6. I have some . . . . news for you. (GOOD)

7. The . . . . thing I must do is phone my friend. (LAST)

8. It's a . . . . journey from here to the mountains. (SHORT)

9. Sandra's boyfriend is . . . . and has brown hair. (SHORT)

10. I usually travel on the . . . . train to the city. (SLOW)

11. All the windows upstairs are . . . . (SHUT)

12. The bus is sometimes . . . . in the winter. (EARLY)

13. How . . . . is Frank's car? (SMALL)

14. Prices are often very . . . . in the summer. (LOW)

15. Now lift your . . . . leg as high as possible. (RIGHT)

16. How many questions did you get . . . . ? (RIGHT)

Suchen Sie aus der obigen Aufgabe Wörter, die das Gegenteil dieser Wörter bedeuten.

17. dear	. . . .	21. hard	. . . .
18. correct	. . . .	22. quick	. . . .
19. freezing	. . . .	23. closed	. . . .
20. huge	. . . .	24. final	. . . .

8.4 Prepositions of place (1)

Präpositionen des Ortes (1)

Schreiben Sie die folgenden Präpositionen unter die Bilder. Benutzen Sie jede Präposition nur ein Mal.

outside	in	at	beside
through	under	over	down
behind	near	on	between

1. . . . . . . the moon
2. . . . . . . the top
3. . . . . . . the car
4. . . . . . . my back
5. . . . . . . the tent
6. . . . . . the keyhole
7. . . . . . . the hill
8. . . . . . . the hurdle
9. . . . . . . Parliament
10. . . . . . . the clock
11. . . . . . . the cars
12. . . . . . . Paris

Prepositions of place (2)

Präpositionen des Ortes (2)

Wählen Sie die richtige Präposition.

1. Brian's staying with a friend . . . . number 6 London Road.
   a. at   b. on   c. up   d. through

2. Go . . . . that road and you'll see a No. 57 bus stop.
   a. between   b. at   c. across   d. around

3. Be careful! Don't fall . . . . the stairs. They're still wet.
   a. to   b. down   c. past   d. opposite

4. Graham sits . . . . Janet and Rita in music lessons.
   a. at   b. among   c. between   d. in

5. Turn left . . . . the traffic lights, then right.
   a. at   b. on   c. into   d. along

6. Walk . . . . the road as far as the park.
   a. at   b. along   c. through   d. around

7. We live . . . . Glasgow, not far from the city centre.
   a. at   b. among   c. in   d. on

8. You'll find the book . . . . the table, under the newspaper.
   a. at   b. in   c. on   d. back to

9. Malcolm lives in a large house . . . . Nelson Avenue.
   a. through   b. in   c. among   d. between

10. The office where I work is . . . . the town centre.
    a. on   b. near   c. along   d. across

11. Put your bag . . . . the chair. It'll be safe there.
    a. at   b. up   c. under   d. past

12. Our flat is . . . . the shop so we don't have far to go to work!
    a. on   b. above   c. back to   d. off

13. Take your feet . . . . the table! Who do you think you are?
    a. in front of b. down   c. not far from d. off

14. The station is . . . . the town centre so leave early!
    a. down   b. on   c. off   d. a long way from

15. Meet me . . . . the bus stop at a quarter to eight.
    a. over   b. at   c. across   d. through

Prepositions of time – at, in, on

Präpositionen der Zeit – at, in, on

Beachten Sie, wie diese drei Präpositionen benutzt werden:

AT	for a **time** – at 6 o'clock
	for a **festival** – at Christmas, Easter, Midsummer
	in the expressions – at night, at the moment, at the weekend
IN	for a **month** – in October
	for a **year** – in 1990
	for a **season** – in autumn, winter, spring, summer
	in the expressions – in the morning/afternoon/evening
ON	for a **day** – on Tuesday, on 2nd July, Christmas Day
	for a **part of a day** – on Saturday morning

Fügen Sie *at*, *in* oder *on* in die Sätze ein.

1. Don't you love getting up late . . . . the weekend?

2. Our neighbours go on holiday . . . . spring.

3. I'd like to travel to Glasgow . . . . 3rd August.

4. I'll see you . . . . the morning.

5. I always go to town to do some shopping . . . . Saturday.

6. It can get cold here . . . . January so bring warm clothes!

7. George is often late . . . . Monday mornings and so is the boss.

8. The last bus goes . . . . midnight and taxis are very expensive.

9. It was nice to meet all my friends . . . . New Year.

10. We usually visit my wife's family . . . . New Year's Day.

11. I think Max was in London for the first time . . . . 1993.

12. Could you take your holiday . . . . September this year?

13. Susie has a lot of work to do . . . . the moment.

14. Would you like to go sailing . . . . Saturday afternoon?

15. The train leaves . . . . 8.45 . . . . the evening.

16. Would you like to go out for dinner . . . . your birthday?

17. We want to give Miranda a surprise party . . . . Friday.

69

Aufgabe 1

Vervollständigen Sie die Sätze mit jeweils einem der folgenden Adverbien.

about	finally	normally	really
fast	hard	quite	slowly

1. Could you speak more . . . . , please? It's difficult for Yoshiko to understand.
2. Are you sure? Do you . . . . want to go away this weekend?
3. Freddy is . . . . tall but not as tall as me.
4. What's the time? < I think it's . . . . one o'clock, but I'm not sure.
5. Don't drive so . . . . ! We're in the centre of town!
6. Steve . . . . gets home about six, but tonight he's going to be a bit late.
7. After waiting for over an hour, we . . . . boarded the plane.
8. I know your exam is next week, but don't work too . . . .

Aufgabe 2

Tun Sie das Gleiche nun mit diesen Adverbien.

carefully	nearly	quickly	usually
immediately	occasionally	unfortunately	well

1. Only a few more miles to go! We're . . . . home.
2. Help! Come . . . . ! I'm going to drop this!
3. I don't want to forget, so I'll do it . . . .
4. I love listening to Jeff play the piano. He plays so . . . .
5. Now watch . . . . I want you to do this in a minute.
6. We . . . . eat out, but not very often.
7. I'd love to come to your party but . . . . I'm out of the country that week.
8. I . . . . take sugar, but I can drink it without.

8.8 Adjective phrases
Adjektivverbindungen

Aufgabe 1

Vervollständigen Sie die Sätze mit jeweils einer der folgenden Adjektivverbindungen.

afraid of	full of	interested in	sure about
engaged to	good at	pleased with	worried about

1. My boss was . . . . my work and put up my salary.
2. What's Martin so . . . . ? < He's taking his driving test tomorrow!
3. Lynda is . . . . Brian. They're getting married next year.
4. I'm not very . . . . cooking but I do my best.
5. We know Paula is coming but we aren't . . . . Judy.
6. Your homework is . . . . mistakes! You must be more careful!
7. Cheryl looks bored. I don't think she's very . . . . ballet.
8. We got to the airport early because we were . . . . missing the plane.

Aufgabe 2

Tun Sie das Gleiche nun mit diesen Verbindungen.

annoyed with	kind of	sorry for	terrified of
fond of	late for	terrible at	wrong with

1. It was very . . . . you to help me. < Not at all.
2. At school I was . . . . English. It was my worst subject.
3. Where's the bus? We're going to be . . . . work.
4. Susan stayed out all night. Her parents were very . . . . her.
5. Something's . . . . this photocopier. It won't work.
6. Harry is very . . . . his grandchildren. He'll do anything for them.
7. Damien is . . . . spiders and jumps every time he sees one.
8. I feel really . . . . Jeremy. He hasn't got any money and he's lost his job.

8.9 Verbs with at/to
Verben mit at/to

Vervollständigen Sie diese Sätze mit *at* oder *to*.

1. Josie's plane gets . . . . New York at ten o'clock.

2. Susan, come and look . . . . these fish in the river.

3. We often go . . . . Macdonald's on Saturday.

4. Charlie comes . . . . work by helicopter every day.

5. People will laugh . . . . you if you wear that silly tie!

6. Susie writes . . . . her boyfriend every day!

7. Can we stop . . . . the supermarket on the way home?

8. I want to give this ring . . . . my favourite granddaughter.

9. Darren only listens . . . . pop music on the radio.

10. I want to talk . . . . you about something very serious.

11. Who does this book belong . . . . ? < I think it's Harry's.

12. We want to arrive . . . . the airport in good time.

13. Throw the ball . . . . the tin and try to knock it down.

14. Muriel prefers living in the town . . . . living in the country.

15. I can't lend my CD player . . . . everybody who asks me!

16. Could you explain this word . . . . me? I can't understand it.

17. What's everybody staring . . . . ? It's only a wasp!

18. Could you pass this note . . . . Miss Johnson?

 Unterstreichen Sie das Verb und die Präposition, um sie sich gemeinsam einzuprägen.

8.10 Verbs with from/for/of/on
Verben mit from/for/of/on

Aufgabe 1

Vervollständigen Sie diese Sätze mit *from* oder *for*.

1. I had no money so I had to borrow some . . . . Jim.

2. The thief stole Mabel's purse . . . . her handbag.

3. Which company do you work . . . . ?

4. Good morning. I'm the manager. What can I do . . . . you?

5. I'm looking . . . . my book. I left it somewhere in this room.

6. The two murderers escaped . . . . prison last night.

7. I'd like to thank you . . . . all your help.

8. Rupert should apologise . . . . being so late.

9. Right, so who is going to pay . . . . the drinks?

10. I'm Dutch. Which country do you come . . . . ?

11. You work too hard! You should ask your boss . . . . a holiday!

Aufgabe 2

Vervollständigen Sie jetzt diese Sätze mit *of* oder *on*.

1. George spends all his money . . . . computer games.

2. Can you think . . . . a word that means the same as "unhappy"?

3. This food reminds me . . . . the time I went to Spain.

4. Are you going to play tennis? < It depends . . . . the weather.

5. It's so noisy in here! I can't concentrate . . . . my work!

Unterstreichen Sie das Verb und die Präposition, um sie sich gemeinsam einzuprägen.

8.11 Prepositional phrases
Präpositionsverbindungen

Aufgabe 1

Vervollständigen Sie diese Sätze mit jeweils einer dieser Verbindungen.

at least	for ages	in a hurry	in private
by air	for example	in love	in time

1. Jo never travels . . . . as she hates flying.
2. Why does Nigel run everywhere? He's always . . . .
3. Luckily we arrived just . . . . to catch the last bus.
4. The organisers expect . . . . 70 people to come to the meeting but there could be many more.
5. Have you got any identification, ... a driving licence?
6. Oh, hello! I haven't seen you . . . . ! How are you?
7. Kevin keeps sending me flowers. I think he must be . . . . !
8. Can I speak to you . . . . ? I don't want the others to hear.

Aufgabe 2

Tun Sie das Gleiche nun mit diesen Sätzen.

out of work	in fact	on foot	on the phone
in his forties	on his own	on holiday	on time

1. We came back . . . . I'm sure the walk was good for us.
2. The plane left . . . . but it arrived an hour late.
3. After the children left, Joe lived . . . . for a few years.
4. I think my boss is . . . . but it's difficult to say exactly how old he is.
5. Ruth is away . . . . at a hotel somewhere in the Bahamas.
6. Is that boy still . . . . ? Who is he talking to now?
7. If the factory closes, 150 people will be . . . .
8. People think he comes from the USA but . . . . he's Canadian.

Link words
Verbindungswörter

In dieser Übung werden Ihnen die Wörter *and*, *but* und *as soon as* begegnen. Man benutzt sie, um zwei Satzteile miteinander zu verbinden.

Aufgabe 1

Ordnen Sie die jeweils passenden Satzhälften einander zu. Tragen Sie Ihre Antworten in die Kästchen ein.

1. The weather was terrible	a. when he saw the mess.	1.	
2. I'm taking my car	b. as soon as I have any news.	2.	
3. Frank didn't go to bed	c. and John is taking his.	3.	
4. I'll phone you	d. before I could answer it.	4.	
5. The phone stopped ringing	e. although he was very tired.	5.	
6. Sally went to bed early	f. so we didn't go out.	6.	
7. My father was very angry	g. because she was so tired.	7.	

Aufgabe 2

Tun Sie das Gleiche nun mit diesen Satzhälften.

1. We're going on holiday to the place	a. so that your students can understand.	1.	
2. You must speak slowly and clearly	b. than her husband does.	2.	
3. Maggie drives much more carefully	c. while I was doing some shopping.	3.	
4. The team played very well	d. until everyone is here.	4.	
5. I met an old friend	e. where we first met.	5.	
6. Angela usually has a shower every morning	f. but they didn't play well enough to win the match.	6.	
7. We can't start this meeting	g. after she has breakfast.	7.	

Unterstreichen Sie alle Verbindungswörter, und schreiben Sie Sätze, in denen sie vorkommen.

8.13 One word – two uses

Ein Wort – zwei Verwendungsmöglicheiten

Manche Wörter können sowohl Nomen wie auch Verb sein. Das Wort *walk* ist hierfür ein gutes Beispiel:

Why don't you walk to the station. It isn't far.   Hier ist *walk* ein Verb.
Let's go for a walk. It's a lovely afternoon.   Hier ist *walk* ein Nomen.

Hier sind einige Wörter, die sowohl Verb als auch Nomen sein können. Benutzen Sie das jeweilige Wort zur Vervollständigung der Satzpaare.

answer	dream	drive	help	phone
plan	promise	queue	rain	visit

1. a. Every night I . . . . about the girl I met on holiday.

   b. Cathy had a horrible . . . . about falling out of a plane.

2. a. We had to . . . . for hours to get tickets for the concert.

   b. There was already a long . . . . when we got to the theatre.

3. a. Trudy's gone to Manchester to . . . . her grandparents.

   b. Mike's away on a . . . . to his uncle in Madrid.

4. a. I'll give you my home number so you can . . . . me there.

   b. Is Mandy still on the . . . . ? I've got a call to make!

5. a. Could you . . . . me to carry these boxes to the car?

   b. Do you need any . . . . with the washing-up?

6. a. Look at those clouds! I'm sure it's going to . . . .

   b. The . . . . came down so heavily that we had to go inside.

7. a. June didn't learn to . . . . a car until she was thirty.

   b. Let's go for a . . . . in the country this afternoon.

8. a. Don't just live for today. You must . . . . for the future.

   b. The . . . . of the hotel will show you where the pool is.

9. a. You will come, won't you? < Yes, I will. I . . . .

   b. Hamish didn't come. He didn't keep his . . . .

10. a. . . . . my question! Who was that girl you were with?

    b. Jim wrote the company a letter but he never got an . . . .

76

9. Kapitel

Word Puzzles
Wortspiele

1. Englisch macht Spaß.

Wenn Sie beim Lernen keinen Spaß haben, werden Sie nicht viel lernen! Wenn Sie etwas langweilig finden, hören Sie damit auf! Man lernt am besten, wenn man interessiert und engagiert ist.

2. Wenn Sie Spaß an Wortspielen haben, versuchen Sie, sich mehr davon zu beschaffen.

Alle Wortspiele helfen beim Erlernen von Vokabular. Je mehr Sie davon machen, umso mehr Wörter werden Sie lernen.

9.1 Verb snake

Die Verbschlange

Vervollständigen Sie die Schlange mit den Verben, die Sie in die Sätze einfügen. Der letzte Buchstabe eines Verbs ist gleichzeitig der erste Buchstabe des folgenden einzufügenden Verbs.

draw	know	lend	phone	stop	travel
drop	laugh	need	pull	tell	wait
help	learn	pass	put	thank	want

1. How can I make this room more fun to live in?
   < . . . . some posters up!

2. We want to . . . . you for all your help.

3. What's the time? < I'm afraid I don't . . . .

4. I usually . . . . for the bus outside the post office.

5. Sally hopes to . . . . around America one day.

6. I don't think that programme is funny. Other people
   . . . . at it but not me!

7. Can you . . . . me to move this, please. I can't do it by myself.

8. If you push the table, I'll . . . . it.

9. Ivor would like to . . . . another language.

10. Do you . . . . some more water to wash the window?

11. Could you . . . . me a map to show me the way to your house?

12. I don't . . . . to go to bed! I'm not tired!

13. Could you . . . . me the time? < Yes, it's ten o'clock.

14. Could you . . . . me your pen? Mine doesn't work.

15. Be careful with those glasses! Don't . . . . them!

16. Could you . . . . me the salt, please?

17. Please . . . . talking. I'm trying to think.

18. I want to . . . . James. What's his number?

Odd one out

Welches Wort gehört hier nicht hin?

Eins der vier Wörter paßt nicht in die jeweilige Liste. Warum? Falls Sie Probleme haben, suchen Sie sich die Begründung aus dem Kasten unter der Übung aus.

The others:

1. aunt   daughter   mother   (nephew)   *are women/female*
2. bathroom bedroom   garden   kitchen   . . . .
3. beer   cake   coffee   tea   . . . .
4. twelve   sixty   twice   sixteen   . . . .
5. eyes   knee   mouth   nose   . . . .
6. Ecuador   German   Spain   Zambia   . . . .
7. drums   goal   guitar   piano   . . . .
8. bicycle   bus   car   lorry   . . . .
9. football   hockey   judo   photography . . . .
10. autumn   summer   weekend   winter   . . . .
11. breakfast dinner   lemon   lunch   . . . .
12. afternoon evening   journey   morning   . . . .
13. cup   glass   mug   plate   . . . .
14. bird   cat   dog   horse   . . . .
15. rain   snow   spring   wind   . . . .
16. cigar   cigarette   pipe   ice cream . . . .
17. forest   lake   river   sea   . . . .
18. cooker   fridge   grill   shower   . . . .
19. boots   gloves   shoes   slippers . . . .
20. book   film   magazine newspaper . . . .

The others

a. can't fly   b. have four wheels   c. are countries   d. are in the kitchen

e. are inside a house   f. are meals   g. are musical instruments   h. are numbers

i. are on the face   j. are parts of the day   k. are seasons   l. are sports

m. are types of weather   n. are water   o. are women/female

p. are things you drink   q. are things you read   r. are things you smoke

s. are things you use to drink   t. are things you wear on your feet

Verb square (1)
Verbquadrat (1)

Suchen Sie in dem Wortquadrat die Vergangenheitsformen dieser Verben.

break	forget	lend	run	stop	think
cut	hide	make	shut	swim	try
fall	is	meet	sleep	take	wear
find	leave	put	spend	tell	win

Die Wörter können waagerecht, senkrecht oder diagonal nach rechts und links stehen. Ein Buchstabe kann gleichzeitig in mehreren Wörtern vorkommen.

S	P	E	N	T	R	I	E	D	T
T	U	B	W	S	W	A	M	R	H
M	T	C	R	A	N	W	F	S	O
A	E	U	B	O	S	O	O	T	U
D	N	T	O	O	K	R	R	O	G
E	L	E	N	T	I	E	G	P	H
S	W	F	S	A	N	N	O	P	T
H	O	E	I	L	E	F	T	E	H
U	N	L	S	L	E	P	T	D	I
T	O	L	D	D	F	O	U	N	D

 Wenn Sie ein Verb lernen, überprüfen Sie, ob es sich um ein unregelmäßiges Verb handelt. Denken Sie auch daran, daß einige Verben, deren Vergangenheitsformen auf *-ed* enden, anders buchstabiert werden, z. B.:

cry	cried	permit	permitted

Ein gutes Wörterbuch weist auf solche Veränderungen hin.

Verb square (2)

Verbquadrat (2)

Suchen Sie in dem Wortquadrat die Vergangenheitsformen dieser Verben.

begin	do	feel	have	read	see
buy	drink	get	hear	ride	sing
can	drive	give	know	ring	sit
come	eat	go	pay	say	write

Die Wörter können waagerecht, senkrecht oder diagonal nach rechts und links stehen. Ein Buchstabe kann gleichzeitig in mehreren Wörtern vorkommen.

G	O	T	K	E	C	O	U	L	D
B	E	G	A	N	F	D	I	D	Y
I	C	A	T	N	E	W	H	R	C
R	O	V	E	A	L	W	A	A	A
E	S	E	O	S	T	E	D	N	M
A	A	A	O	A	S	R	S	K	E
D	W	E	N	T	O	P	A	I	D
Y	B	O	U	G	H	T	I	N	E
D	R	O	V	E	R	O	D	E	G
H	E	A	R	D	W	R	O	T	E

Übrigens: Es gibt nur etwa 100 wichtige unregelmäßige Verben im Englischen. Diese gehören allerdings zu den gebräuchlichsten aller Wörter.

Crossword (1)

Kreuzworträtsel (1)

Vervollständigen Sie die Sätze und tragen Sie die gefundenen Begriffe in das Kreuzworträtsel ein. Die fehlenden Wörter sind unterhalb des Kreuzworträtsels abgedruckt. Versuchen Sie aber zunächst das Rätsel zu lösen, ohne sich die Wörter anzusehen.

ACROSS

1. Sally's father was so . . . . when she crashed his car!
3. I'm very . . . . Shall we have something to drink?
5. It was . . . . to see so many of my old friends again.
6. Smoking is . . . . , but a lot of people smoke anyway.
8. It's getting . . . . in here. Could you switch the light on?
9. There's some really . . . . countryside in this part of the world.
11. Let's leave as early as . . . . in the morning.
13. Mark's quite tall, with . . . . hair and brown eyes.
15. . . . . New Year!
16. I've just washed this shirt but it's still . . . .
17. I'm not really . . . . in reading. I prefer sport.
20. There are more people here than we expected. I'll get some . . . . chairs.
21. Are you . . . . on Monday? We're all going bowling.
22. This dress is too . . . . for me. Have you got a smaller size?
23. We live in a very . . . . part of town.
24. It's . . . . to explain what the problem is, but I'll try.

DOWN

1. Do you know where Bill is? < No, I'm . . . . not.
2. Let's go for a walk. < . . . . idea!
3 There's been a . . . . accident! Three people are dead.
4. This dictionary is much more . . . . than my old one.
7. We always go to a disco. Let's go somewhere . . . . for a change.
10. Carol is so . . . . She leaves her things all over the floor!

12. We must speak to Mrs Parker at once. It's very . . . .

14. It was very cold last night so the roads are . . . . this morning.

15. The coffee's too . . . . so I'll leave it for a minute.

18. I'm . . . . I had a late night last night.

19. Isn't Canberra the capital of Australia? < Yes, that's . . . .

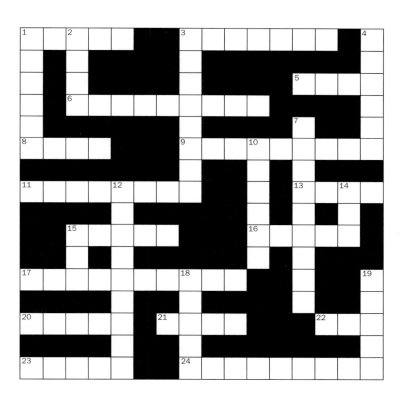

afraid, angry, beautiful, big, dangerous, dark, different, difficult, dirty, extra, fair, free, good, happy, hot, icy, important, interested, nice, possible, quiet, right, terrible, thirsty, tired, untidy, useful

Crossword (2)

Kreuzworträtsel (2)

Vervollständigen Sie die Sätze, und tragen Sie die gefundenen Begriffe in das Kreuzworträtsel ein. Die fehlenden Wörter sind unterhalb des Kreuzworträtsels abgedruckt. Versuchen Sie aber zunächst das Rätsel zu lösen, ohne sich die Wörter anzusehen.

ACROSS

1. Have you read ". . . . . the World in 80 Days"?
4. There's . . . . wrong with the car. It won't start.
8. What was the game . . . . ? < Not bad.
9. I hurt . . . . leg while I was playing football.
10. Please sit . . . . Can I get you something to drink?
12. Did Mary lend you the money? < No, ... didn't.
14. The train leaves . . . . six o'clock.
16. Is Brian coming with us? I think . . . .
18. Their new . . . . has five bedrooms and three bathrooms.
21. What does 'terrified' . . . . ? < Very frightened.
22. Do you know who . . . . girls are over there?
24. 1994 was a very important . . . . in my life.
25. I've got so much to . . . . this week.
26. More tea? < . . . . please.
28. Can I come in? < Of . . . . you can.
29. A coffee, please. < With or . . . . milk?
34. Is it . . . . snowing? < No. It stopped about five minutes ago.
36. My alarm didn't ring so I got . . . . late.
37. I waited . . . . that bus for half an hour yesterday!
38. Who wants the . . . . piece of cake?
40. How . . . . is Pat? < In her thirties, I think.
41. How long does it . . . . you to get to work? < About an hour.
42. Are you sure you . . . . want to be a soldier?
43. Would you like . . . . biscuit? < No, thanks. One is enough.

DOWN

1. We played . . . . a team which was much better than ours.
2. The tickets are very cheap. They're . . . . a pound.
3. What . . . . Joe do in his spare time? < As little as possible!
4. Oh no! That woman's wearing the . . . . dress as I am!
5. The film was so bad that we left before the . . . .
6. . . . . are you? < Fine, thanks. And you?
7. Exactly how many cars has your boss . . . . ? < At least six.
11. So you speak English. What . . . . languages do you know?

13. I'll tell you . . . . soon as I can.
15. What's . . . . matter? < I've got a headache.
16. He . . . . he loves me but does he really mean it?
17. Which coat is yours? < The dark blue . . . .
19. Put your bag . . . . the seat. It should be safe there.
20. The Smiths went . . . . Germany for their holiday.
21. . . . . I borrow your dictionary?
23. It was . . . . a nice day that we decided to go for a walk.
27. Some . . . . spend lots of money on clothes but Bill doesn't.
28. Have you got any . . . . ? < Yes, two boys.
29. The . . . . gets smaller every year.
30. Could you come . . . . .way, please?
31. Don't forget to switch the computer . . . .
32. It takes about five minutes to drive . . . . the tunnel.
33. Now I live in London, but I . . . . to live in New York.
35. My Spanish is good but I only speak a . . . . Italian.
39. This exercise is more difficult . . . . the other one.

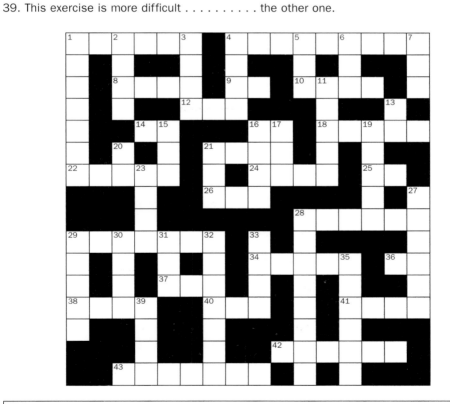

against, another, around, as, at, children, course, do, does, down, end, for, got, house, how, last, like, little, may, mean, my, old, one, only, other, people, really, same, says, she, so, something, still, such, take, than, the, this, those, through, to, under, up, used, without, world, year, yes

Word ladder
Wortleiter

Verwandeln Sie das Wort auf der obersten Sprosse der Leiter in das Wort, das ganz unten steht. Sie dürfen bei jeder Sprosse nur einen Buchstaben des vorherigen Wortes verändern. Wenn Ihnen das gesuchte Wort unbekannt ist, raten Sie und überprüfen Ihre Annahme in Ihrem Wörterbuch. Raten und die Benutzung eines guten Wörterbuches sind wichtige Schritte auf dem Weg zu guten Englischkenntnissen.

1. Go on foot. **WALK**

2. I want to . . . . to you about something.

3. Not short.

4. There's a big . . . . around the house.

5. Don't climb that tree. You might . . . .

6. Your glass is empty. Shall I . . . . it?

7. . . . . you be coming tomorrow? < No, I won't.

8. The shop is at the top of the . . . .

9. The match is in the gymnastics . . . .

10. I'll be back in . . . . an hour.

11. He wanted us to stop so he shouted, ". . . . . !"

12. Put more . . . . in the soup to give it flavour.

13. Don't buy it now! It'll be cheaper in the . . . .

14. Not female.

15. 1.61 kilometres **MILE**

Test 1

Test 1

Wissen Sie noch alles, was Sie gelernt haben? In den nächsten fünf Tests können Sie sich prüfen.

Wählen Sie das jeweils beste Wort.

1. We . . . . TV for most of the evening.
   a. looked   b. looked for   c. saw   d. watched

2. We'll have to use the stairs. The lift is . . . . order.
   a. in   b. out of   c. outside   d. without

3. You'll feel much better, if you . . . . smoking.
   a. get on   b. get out   c. give in   d. give up

4. We were stuck in a traffic . . . . for over an hour.
   a. jam   b. light   c. line   d. stop

5. Flight 547 to Manchester is now ready for . . . .
   a. boarding   b. entering   c. flying   d. leaving

6. Who's going to help me . . . . the balloons for the party?
   a. blow down   b. blow up   c. get down   d. get up

7. Steve plays the . . . . in a pop group.
   a. concert   b. drums   c. opera   d. tunes

8. This is the biggest football . . . . in the country.
   a. court   b. gym   c. ring   d. stadium

9. There will be . . . . rain during the night.
   a. big   b. great   c. heavy   d. long

10. What would you like to drink? < A . . . . water, please.
    a. cup   b. bottle   c. glass   d. mineral

11. My aunt and . . . . have been married for 20 years now.
    a. boyfriend   b. husband   c. grandson   d. uncle

12. We asked the . . . . at the hotel to get us a taxi.
    a. lawyer   b. receptionist   c. reporter   d. stewardess

13. Sandra was never very good . . . . geography.
    a. at   b. for   c. of   d. to

14. What's your favourite . . . . ? < Physics.
    a. break   b. study   c. studying   d. subject

15. I don't need as many as twenty. Just give me . . . .
    a. a dozen   b. a hundred   c. thirty   d. zero

Test 2

Wählen Sie das jeweils beste Wort.

1. What's the time now? < It's . . . . twelve o'clock.
    a. at   b. near   c. nearly   d. most

2. Did you hear the news . . . . the radio?
    a. at   b. by   c. in   d. on

3. Surely Pete can't do all that work . . . . his own!
    a. by   b. for   c. on   d. with

4. Sally's got an office . . . . the fifth floor.
    a. at   b. by   c. in   d. on

5. I'm going to the . . . . to get my new glasses.
    a. artist's   b. engineer's   c. mechanic's   d. optician's

6. Excuse me, are you the . . . . of this bicycle?
    a. customer   b. driver   c. manager   d. owner

7. Could you . . . . a picture of us with my camera?
    a. do   b. give   c. make   d. take

8. I'd like to book two . . . . rooms and one double, please.
    a. alone   b. only   c. single   d. singular

9. Call a . . . . There's water coming through the ceiling.
    a. nurse   b. plumber   c. priest   d. sailor

10. My dog was very ill so I took him to a . . . .
    a. dentist   b. engineer   c. mechanic   d. vet

11. It wasn't very far so we decided to go . . . . foot.
    a. at   b. on   c. to   d. with

12. The Smiths got the car . . . . from Dover to Calais.
    a. ferry   b. journey   c. travel   d. voyage

13. Why don't people put their rubbish in the litter . . . . ?
    a. bins   b. booths   c. stops   d. vans

14. Can I borrow your . . . . to cut my nails?
    a. comb   b. razor   c. knives   d. scissors

15. I hired a . . . . so that I could film the wedding.
    a. camcorder   b. cassette recorder c. record   d. system

Test 3

Wählen Sie das jeweils beste Wort.

1. The sea conditions are just right for us to go . . . .
   a. cycling   b. skating   c. climbing   d. surfing

2. It's cold outside. Don't forget to take your . . . .
   a. pants   b. scarf   c. shorts   d. suit

3. Try the . . . . trout. It's usually very good.
   a. grilled   b. mashed   c. roast   d. minced

4. That rump . . . . was delicious!
   a. mousse   b. salad   c. steak   d. sole

5. Here's a . . . . for you to put your coat on.
   a. collector   b. cupboard   c. exhibition   d. hanger

6. My driving . . . . said that I was certain to pass my test.
   a. director   b. inspector   c. instructor   d. manager

7. The . . . . of the shop gave me my money back.
   a. host   b. manager   c. operator   d. runner

8. Who was the . . . . of this piece of music?
   a. composer   b. composition   c. translator   d. reporter

9. The word '. . . . .' does not rhyme with the others.
   a. clear   b. wear   c. hear   d. dear

10. That's the friend . . . . car I borrowed.
    a. he's   b. whose   c. who's   d. his

11. It was a very serious illness and Max still feels very . . . .
    a. fair   b. faulty   c. soft   d. weak

12. Business people usually . . . . hands when they first meet.
    a. have   b. shake   c. lock   d. hold

13. Let's . . . . the bell and see if she's in.
    a. knock   b. listen to   c. play   d. ring

14. I've . . . . my mind. I think I'll stay at home this evening.
    a. changed   b. done   c. made   d. thought

15. Can we stop for a minute? These suitcases are very . . . .
    a. careful   b. empty   c. heavy   d. tired

Test 4

Wählen Sie das jeweils beste Wort.

1. You look tired. Why don't you have a . . . . ?
   a. lie   b. rest   c. stay   d. stop

2. . . . . care when you bring that dish. It's hot.
   a. Be   b. Have   c. Make   d. Take

3. Kyoko soon made . . . . with the other people in the class.
   a. friend   b. friends   c. friendly   d. friendship

4. You need a . . . . personality to do well in this job.
   a. high   b. weak   c. strong   d. thick

5. The fog was so . . . . that we couldn't see where
   we were going.
   a. big   b. great   c. strong   d. thick

6. The policeman asked to see my . . . . licence.
   a. drive   b. auto   c. driver   d. driving

7. You must show your . . . . card if you want to get in.
   a. identical   b. identify   c. identifying   d. identity

8. The weather . . . . said it would be sunny on Saturday.
   a. forecast   b. news   c. record   d. story

9. Could you pass me the butter? < Certainly. Here . . . .
   a. are you   b. you are   c. is it   d. there is

10. Sorry I'm late. < That's all right. It . . . .
    a. doesn't matter   b. doesn't miss   c. does nothing   d. goes well

11. How much bread do we need? < Just a small . . . .
    a. bake   b. cook   c. loaf   d. stuff

12. And what would you like for the . . . . course, sir?
    a. big   b. great   c. main   d. principal

13. . . . . the third on the right, just after the bank.
    a. Get   b. Go   c. Take   d. Turn

14. Have you got . . . . ? < I'm afraid not. I don't smoke.
    a. fire   b. a fire   c. lighter   d. a light

15. Our plane should . . . . in about half an hour.
    a. go up   b. lend   c. put up   d. take off

Test 5

Wählen Sie das jeweils beste Wort.

1. Turn right . . . . the traffic lights and you'll see the cinema.
   a. at   b. off   c. on   d. over

2. I rented a house . . . . Suffolk Avenue.
   a. among   b. between   c. in   d. through

3. Did you do anything special . . . . the weekend?
   a. at   b. in   c. on   d. to

4. Could you meet me . . . . Friday afternoon?
   a. at   b. in   c. on   d. to

5. I . . . . have toast but I wasn't very hungry this morning.
   a. nearly   b. normally   c. quite   d. well

6. This letter is full . . . . mistakes. Could you do it again, please?
   a. from   b. in   c. of   d. with

7. Tricia is really fond . . . . Andy. Did you see the
   present she gave him?
   a. for   b. of   c. on   d. with

8. Pat's still . . . . the phone. Who is she talking to?
   a. in   b. on   c. over   d. to

9. Charles has been out of . . . . for over a year now.
   a. employ   b. employed   c. job   d. work

10. I'll call you . . . . I have any news.
    a. as soon   b. as soon as   c. soonest   d. while

11. I'm very . . . . Is there anything cool to drink?
    a. dirty   b. hunger   c. hungry   d. thirsty

12. Can you come to the meeting? < No, I'm . . . . not.
    a. afraid   b. sorry   c. sure   d. think

13. Joe's not really very . . . . in the theatre. He
    prefers the cinema.
    a. excited   b. interested   c. fond   d. keen

14. It . . . . me about an hour to get to work.
    a. gets   b. makes   c. spends   d. takes

15 What's the . . . . ? < I can't find my wallet.
    a. halt   b. matter   c. stop   d. wrong

Answers

Lösungsschlüssel

1.2   1.c 2.b 3.f 4.g 5.i 6.e 7.a 8.h 9.d

1.3   catch, fare

1.4   1.speak English 2.do your homework 3.have a bath 4.make a mistake 5.play golf 6.ride a bike 7.catch a bus 8.watch TV 9.catch a bus 10.speak English 11.play golf 12.watch TV

1.5   1.friendly 2.swimming 3.dangerous 4.painting 5.information 6.windy

1.6   1.one, brother, come, front, love, money 2.hot, copy, job, long, often, stop 3.go, close, home, most, open, show

1.7   1.hurry 2.delicious 3.artist 4.of course 5.give up 6.department store 7.terrible 8.out of order 9.recommend 10.shampoo

1.8   1.traffic, passport, flight, travel 2.leave, take, miss, board 3.in, through, from 4.at, in, for 5.man, hair, glasses 6.up, up, up 7.Can, down, like

1.9   1.tall and thin 2.thin and bald 3.tired and sleepy 4.old and poor 5.nice and tasty 6.short and fat 7.young and happy 8.tired and dirty 9.wet and windy 10.rich and famous 11.nice and sunny 12.hot and angry

2.1   1.furniture: armchair, bed, chair, sofa, stool, table 2.family: brother-in-law, cousin, grandson, nephew, parents, uncle 3.colours: black, blue, green, red, white, yellow 4.music: concert, drums, opera singer, play a tune, pop song, violin

2.2   1.sport: baseball team, football stadium, play volleyball, referee, tennis court, win the match 2.drinks: bottle of wine, cup of coffee, glass of milk, lemonade, mineral water, orange juice 3.clothes: blouse, long skirt, pair of socks, pair of trousers, smart suit, warm coat 4.weather: heavy rain, temperature, shower, sunny, sunshine, windy

2.3   **Days**: 1.Monday 2.Tuesday 3.Wednesday 4.Thursday 5.Friday 6.Saturday 7.Sunday   **Parts of a day**: 1.morning 2.afternoon 3.evening 4.night **Months**: 1.January 2.February 3.March 4.April 5.May 6.June 7.July 8.August 9.September 10.October 11.November 12.December   **Seasons**: 1.spring 2.summer 3.autumn 4.winter   **Time**: 1.second 2.minute 3.hour 4.day 5.week 6.month 7.year

2.4   **Men**: husband, uncle, prince, nephew, boyfriend, grandfather, king, grandson **Women**: wife, grandmother, granddaughter, aunt, princess, niece, widow, queen, girlfriend   **Both**: teacher, violinist, detective, lawyer, receptionist, manager, tourist, dancer, reporter, pilot, artist, engineer, mechanic

2.5   **Subjects:** geography, mathematics, physics   **Things:** desk, dictionary, ruler **Places:** primary school, secondary school   **People:** headmistress, schoolteacher, student   **Verbs:** take, translate   **Other:** good/bad at, lunch break

3.1   **Aufgabe 1** 1.19; 2.18; 3.87; 4.11; 5.54; 6.43; 7.14; 8.100; 9.12; 10.98; 11.1.5; 12.17; 13.76; 14.65; 15.32; 16.1,000; 17.21; 18.$2^1/_2$; 19.212; 20.0; 21.3,679; 22.1,300,010   **Aufgabe 2** 1.first 2.second 3.third 4.fourth 5.fifth 6.eighth 7.ninth 8.twelfth 9.fifteenth 10.twentieth 11.twenty-third 12.twenty-seventh 13.thirtieth 14.thirty-first

3.2   **Aufgabe 1** 1.1969, nineteen sixty-nine 2.1789, seventeen eighty-nine 3.1945, nineteen forty-five 4.1989, nineteen eighty-nine   **Aufgabe 2** 1.the first of January 2.February the twenty-ninth 3.the fourth of July 4.December the twenty-fourth

3.3 1.nine o'clock 2.six thirty 3.(a) quarter to seven 4.two ten 5.eleven fifty 6.three fifteen 7.twenty-five past one 8.five to one 9.five thirty-five 10.nearly quarter past four 11.just after seven forty 12.almost five past three

3.4 **Aufgabe 1** 1.f 2.a 3.h 4.g 5.i 6.d 7.b 8.c **Aufgabe 2** 1.i 2.c 3.a 4.b 5.g 6.d 7.f 8.h

3.5 1.b 2.d 3.a 4.b 5.d 6.b 7.d 8.a 9.a 10.a 11.b 12.c 13.c 14.a

3.6 1.cowboy 2.guitar 3.violin 4.referee 5.stadium 6.shorts 7.penalty 8.lose 9.take 10.camera 11.video 12.horror

3.7 1.receptionist 2.single room 3.caravan 4.bike 5.airport 6.train 7.restaurant 8.disco 9.yacht 10.swimming 11.pool 12.credit card 13.guide book 14.suitcase 15.aspirin

3.8 1.doctor 2.nurse 3.pilot 4.cook 5.teacher 6.sailor 7.priest 8.vet 9.footballer 10.waiter 11.librarian 12.taxi driver 13.car mechanic 14.hairdresser 15.office worker 16.lorry driver 17.shop assistant 18.tourist guide 19.plumber 20.factory worker

3.9 1.We flew. 2.We went by bus. 3.We took a taxi. 4.We came by train. 5.We hired a car. 6.We came on foot. 7.We got the car ferry. 8.We came on our bikes. 9.We took the underground. 1.by plane 2.coaches 3.by boat 4.walk 5.cycle

3.10 1.I got up at 7.30. 2.I had a shower. 3.I waited for the bus. 4.I had a meeting at 9. 5.I went to the dentist. 6.I met Mark for lunch. 7.I was busy all afternoon. 8.We had dinner. 9.We kissed goodnight. After have: have a shower, have a meeting, have dinner. The following can follow have: a sandwich, a headache, a good time, a coffee, a problem, an idea, a bad throat, a beer. "cold" and "hunger" can't follow HAVE.

3.11 1.bike 2.crossing 3.bus stop 4.road sign 5.lorry 6.van 7.litter bin 8.pavement 9.policeman 10.traffic lights 11.public toilet (loo) 12.phone box 13.motorbike 14.lamp post 15.pram

3.12 1.clock 2.pen 3.key 4.wallet 5.credit card 6.calculator 7.toothbrush 8.glasses 9.pencil 10.watch 11.comb 12.notes 13.cheque 14.file 15.contact lenses 16.coins 17.magazine 18.scissors 19.envelope 20.stamp

3.13 1.mobile phone 2.headphones 3.radio/cassette recorder 4.car stereo 5.camera 6.camcorder 7.personal CD 8.personal stereo 9.stereo system

3.14 1.apple 2.cherries 3.pineapple 4.orange 5.lemon 6.grapes 7.pear 8.peach 9.banana 10.peas 11.cabbage 12.potatoes 13.carrot 14.beans 15.onions 16.lettuce 17.cucumber 18.tomatoes

3.15 1.football 2.tennis 3.golf 4.skiing 5.skating 6.cycling 7.fishing 8.sailing 9.windsurfing 10.swimming 11.table tennis 12.surfing 13.riding 14.basketball 15.American football

3.16 1.shirt 2.shoe 3.socks 4.trainers 5.dress 6.skirt 7.bra 8.tights 9.anorak 10.coat 11.jacket 12.track-suit 13.jeans 14.scarf 15.suit 16.trousers 17.cap 18.T-shirt 19.boots 20.shorts 21.jumper/sweater/pullover 22.hat 23.knickers/pants 24.underpants

3.17 **Starters:** vegetable soup, fruit juice **Fish/shellfish:** lobster, grilled trout, Scottish salmon, sole **Meat:** lamb cutlets, rump steak, roast chicken, roast pork **Vegetables:** cauliflower, peas, beans, carrots **Potatoes:** roast potatoes, baked potato, mashed potato, French fries **Desserts:** ice cream, chocolate mousse, apple pie, yoghurt, fruit salad

4.1 1.careful 2.sunny 3.surprised 4.surprising 5.funny 6.worried 7.stormy 8.married 9.interesting 10.wonderful 11.beautiful 12.sleepy 13.useful 14.embarrassed 15.tiring 16.excited

4.2 1.cooker 2.building 3.information 4.meaning 5.recorder 6.beginning 7.shopping 8.exhibition 9.hanger 10.smoking 11.maker 12.direction 13.meeting 14.translation 15.freezer 16.heating 17.collection 18.painting

4.3 1.actor 2.baker 3.collector 4.director 5.driver 6.farmer 7.gardener 8.inspector 9.instructor 10.manager 11.operator 12.player 13.reporter 14.rider 15.runner 16.sailor 17.teacher 18.translator 19.visitor 20.worker 1.driver 2.manager 3.collector 4.reporter 5.player/manager 6.instructor

4.4 **-an:** Brazilian, Canada, German, Hungary, Mexican, Russia   **-ish:** Finnish, Ireland, Polish, Scotland, Spanish, Turkey   **-ese:** Chinese, Japan, Lebanese, Portugal, Taiwanese, Vietnam   **others:** French, Greece, Omani, Switzerland, Thai, Wales

4.5 1.flying 2.daily 3.illness 4.anger 5.composer 6.faulty 7.politician 8.stormy 9.possibilities 10.shorten 11.healthy, healthy 12.hearing

5.1 1.shop, top, want, what 2.boot, new, two, you 3.chair, their, wear, where 4.make, rain, steak, they 5.cheer, dear, here, near 6. know, phone, toast, toe

5.2 1.a.too b.two 2.a.son b.sun 3.a.sea b.see 4.a.it's b.its 5.a.buy b.by 6.a.hear b.here 7.a.right b.write 8.a.who's b.whose

5.3 1.a.passed b.past 2.a.knew b.new 3.a.their b.there 4.a.hour b.our 5.a.wood b.would 6.a.meat b.meet 7.a.weak b.week 8.a.some b.sum 9.a.there b.they're 10.a.fair b.fare 11.a.pair b.pear 12.a.wait b.weight

5.4 1.shall 2.own 3.well 4.move 5.cow 6.phone 7.coat 8.pear 9.here 10.cost 11.after 12.eat 13.shout 14.tea 15.no 16.warm 17.said 18.white

5.5 1.April, breakfast, easy, husband, sweater, traffic 2.again, begin, between, enjoy, hotel, Japan 3.certainly, difficult, holiday, hospital, manager, telephone 4.another, banana, December, eleven, example, musician

6.1 **Aufgabe 1** 1.d 2.f 3.e 4.b 5.a 6.c 7.h 8.g   **Aufgabe 2** 1.e 2.a 3.g 4.h 5.d 6.c 7.b 8.f; 1.shake hands 2.wear glasses 3.post a letter 4.improve your English

6.2 **Aufgabe 1** 1.a 2.e 3.d 4.c 5.g 6.h 7.b 8.f **Aufgabe 2** 1.c 2.b 3.e 4.d 5.g 6.h 7.f 8.a; 1.sunny day 2.comfortable chair 3.long time 4.silly mistake

6.3 **Aufgabe 1** 1.read 2.eat 3.paint 4.ride 5.write 6.smile 7.dance 8.miss 9.drink 10.throw 11.open 12.walk **Aufgabe 2** 1.open 2.paint 3.eat 4.read 5.throw 6.ride 7.write/read 8.miss

6.4 **Aufgabe 1** 1.drive 2.sing 3.wash 4.cut 5.draw 6.fall 7.close 8.jump 9.kick 10.run 11.climb 12.cry **Aufgabe 2** 1.wash 2.sing 3.drive 4.draw 5.kick 6.climb 7.cut 8.close

6.5 1.shower 2.rest 3.cold 4.idea 5.difficulty 6.mistake 7.noise 8.cake 9.friends 10.call 11.time 12.seat 13.picture 14.taxi 15.care

6.6 1.beautiful 2.long 3.cold 4.strong 5.thick 6.high 7.funny 8.big 9.old 10.great

6.7 1.d 2.h 3.g 4.j 5.f 6.b 7.i 8.m 9.o 10.k 11.c 12.a 13.l 14.e 15.n 1.summer holiday 2.ice cream 3.weather forecast 4.ground floor

7.1 1.Yes, I am. Can I help you? 2.Nothing special. Why? 3.Thank you. The same to you. 4. Certainly. Here you are. 5. That's all right. It doesn't matter. 6.Thank you. It's nice to be here. 7.Oh no! What shall we do? 8.She doesn't feel very well.

7.2 1.g 2.e 3.h 4.f 5.j 6.i 7.d 8.c 9.a 10.b

7.3 **1. Gespräch** 1.Are you ready 2.What would you like 3.soup of the day 4.for me, too 5.I'd like
2. Gespräch 1.I'm very sorry 2.What a pity 3.How would you like it 4.something to drink 5.Thank you very much

7.4   **1. Gespräch** 1.Excuse me 2.Could you tell me the way 3.Pardon 4.I'm afraid not 5.Why don't you ask 6.Good idea   **2. Gespräch** 1.how to get to 2.of course 3.turn left 4.the second on the right 5.just after a supermarket 6.You're welcome

7.5   **Aufgabe 1** 1.h 2.g 3.f 4.e 5.b 6.c 7.a 8.d
           Aufgabe 2 1.g 2.f 3.a 4.b 5.h 6.e 7.c 8.d

8.1   **Aufgabe 1** 1.babies 2.boxes 3.boys 4.children 5.classes 6.days 7.factories 8.knives 9.leaves 10.lunches 11.men 12.tomatoes 13.teeth 14.women
           Aufgabe 2 1.strawberries 2.lorries 3.buses 4.sandwiches 5.ladies, gentlemen 6.feet

8.2   1.disagree 2.answer 3.lend 4.open 5.go up 6.lose 7.start 8.love 9.take off 10.cry 11.arrive 12.forget 13.buy 14.put on 15.finish/start 16.close/open 17.borrow/lend 18.hate/love 19.find/lose 20.leave/arrive 21.remember/forget 22.sell/buy 23.laugh/cry 24.ask/answer 25.come down/go up 26.take off/put on 27.land/take off 28.agree/disagree

8.3   1.difficult 2.cold 3.new 4.young 5.expensive 6.bad 7.first 8.long 9.tall 10.fast 11.open 12.late 13.big 14.high 15.left 16.wrong 17.cheap 18.wrong 19.hot 20.small 21.easy 22.slow 23.open 24.first

8.4   1.on 2.at 3.under 4.behind 5.in 6.through 7.down 8.over 9.outside 10.beside 11.between 12.near

8.5   1.a 2.c 3.b 4.c 5.a 6.b 7.c 8.c 9.b 10.b 11.c 12.b 13.d 14.d 15.b

8.6   1.at 2.in 3.on 4.in 5.on 6.in 7.on 8.at 9.at 10.on 11.in 12.in 13.at 14.on 15.at, in 16.on 17.on

8.7   **Aufgabe 1** 1.slowly 2.really 3.quite 4.about 5.fast 6.normally 7.finally 8.hard
           Aufgabe 2 1.nearly 2.quickly 3.immediately 4.well 5.carefully 6.occasionally 7.unfortunately 8.usually

8.8   **Aufgabe 1** 1.pleased with 2.worried about 3.engaged to 4.good at 5.sure about 6.full of 7.interested in 8.afraid of   **Aufgabe 2** 1.kind of 2.terrible at 3.late for 4.annoyed with 5.wrong with 6.fond of 7.terrified of 8.sorry for

8.9   1.to 2.at 3.to 4.to 5.at 6.to 7.at 8.to 9.to 10.to 11.to 12.at 13.at 14.to 15.to 16.to 17.at 18.to

8.10   **Aufgabe 1** 1.from 2.from 3.for 4.for 5.for 6.from 7.for 8.for 9.for 10.from 11.for
       Aufgabe 2 1.on 2.of 3.of 4.on 5.on

8.11   **Aufgabe 1** 1.by air 2.in a hurry 3.in time 4.at least 5.for example 6.for ages 7.in love 8.in private   **Aufgabe 2** 1.on foot 2.on time 3.on his own 4.in his forties 5.on holiday 6.on the phone 7.out of work 8.in fact

8.12   **Aufgabe 1** 1.f 2.c 3.e 4.b 5.d 6.g 7.a   **Aufgabe 2** 1.e 2.a 3.b 4.f 5.c 6.g 7.d

8.13   1.dream 2.queue 3.visit 4.phone 5.help 6.rain 7.drive 8.plan 9.promise 10.answer

9.1   1.put 2.thank 3.know 4.wait 5.travel 6.laugh 7.help 8.pull 9.learn 10.need 11.draw 12.want 13.tell 14.lend 15.drop 16.pass 17.stop 18.phone

9.2   1.nephew, o; 2.garden, e; 3.cake, p; 4.twice, h; 5.knee, i; 6.German, c; 7.goal, g; 8.bicycle, b; 9.photography, l; 10.weekend, k; 11.lemon, f; 12.journey, j; 13.plate, s; 14.bird, a; 15.spring, m; 16.ice cream, r; 17.forest, n; 18.shower, d; 19.gloves, t; 20.film, q

9.3/9.4

9.3 Puzzle Solution

9.4 Puzzle Solution

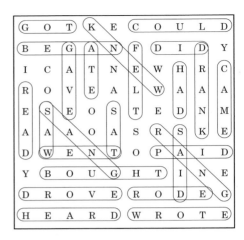

9.5 **Across** 1.angry 3.thirsty 5.nice 6.dangerous 8.dark 9.beautiful 11.possible 13.fair 15.Happy 16.dirty 17.interested 20.extra 21.free 22.big 23.quiet 24.difficult **Down** 1.afraid 2.good 3.terrible 4.useful 7.different 10.untidy 12.important 14.icy 15.hot 18.tired 19.right

9.6 **Across** 1.around 4.something 8.like 9.my 10.down 12.she 14.at 16.so 18.house 21.mean 22.those 24.year 25.do 26.yes 28.course 29.without 34.still 36.up 37.for 38.last 40.old 41.take 42.really 43.another **Down** 1.against 2.only 3.does 4.same 5.end 6.How 7.got 11.other 13.as 15.the 16.says 17.one 19.under 20.to 21.May 23.such 27.people 28.children 29.world 30.this 31.off 32.through 33.used 35.little 39.than

9.7 2.talk 3.tall 4.wall 5.fall 6.fill 7.will 8.hill 9.hall 10.half 11.Halt 12.salt 13.sale 14.male

Test 1 1.d 2.b 3.d 4.a 5.a 6.b 7.b 8.d 9.c 10.d 11.d 12.b 13.a 14.d 15.a

Test 2 1.c 2.d 3.c 4.d 5.d 6.d 7.d 8.c 9.b 10.d 11.b 12.a 13.a 14.d 15.a

Test 3 1.d 2.b 3.a 4.c 5.d 6.c 7.b 8.a 9.b 10.b 11.d 12.b 13.d 14.a 15.c

Test 4 1.b 2.d 3.b 4.c 5.d 6.d 7.d 8.a 9.b 10.a 11.c 12.c 13.c 14.d 15.d

Test 5 1.a 2.c 3.a 4.c 5.b 6.c 7.b 8.b 9.d 10.b 11.d 12.a 13.b 14.d 15.b

Glossary
Alphabetisches Glossar

Dieses Wörterverzeichnis enthält in alphabetischer Reihenfolge Wörter und Redewendungen aus den Kapiteln 1 bis 9 sowie den Tests 1 bis 5. Der Wortschatz des Waystage-Level wird als bekannt vorausgesetzt.
In der linken Spalte befinden sich die Einträge; unregelmäßige Verben sind mit * gekennzeichnet. Die mittlere Spalte gibt die Fundstellen zu den jeweiligen Stichwörtern an, z. B. 8.7 = Kapitel 8 Übung 7. Die deutschen Übersetzungen beziehen sich auf den Kapitel-Kontext, in dem die Einträge zum ersten Mal vorkommen. Wörter, die in unterschiedlichen Bedeutungen auftreten, werden mehrfach genannt.

a light	7.5	Feuer (für Zigarette)	bald	1.9	glatzköpfig
about	8.7	etwa	ballet	8.8	Ballett
above	5.4	oben, darüber	banana	3.14	Banane
accident	4.3	Unfall	baseball team	2.2	Baseball-Mannschaft
act	4.3	Theater spielen	basketball	3.4	Basketball
actor	3.6	Schauspieler	bean	3.14	Bohne
actress	3.6	Schauspielerin	beautiful	6.6	wunderschön
adjective	1.2	Adjektiv, Eigenschaftswort	beauty	4.1	Schönheit
			beginner	3.5	Anfänger/in
alarm	9.6	Wecker	belief	6.6	Glaube
alone	Test 2	allein	bell	6.1	Glocke
along	8.5	entlang	belong	8.9	gehören
American	3.2	Amerikaner/in	beside	8.4	neben
angry	1.9	ärgerlich	bike	1.4	(Fahr)rad
annoyed with	8.8	verärgert über	birthday	3.2	Geburtstag
anorak	3.16	Anorak	birthday card	5.2	Geburtstagskarte
apologise	8.10	sich entschuldigen	biscuit	9.6	Keks
apple	3.14	Apfel	blonde	6.2	blond
armchair	2.1	Sessel	blood	3.6	Blut
around	8.5	herum	blow* down	Test 1	umwehen
arrive	1.8	ankommen	blow* up	1.8	in die Luft sprengen
artist	1.7	Künstler/in	blow* up	Test 1	aufblasen
as … as	8.3	so … wie	board	1.8	an Bord gehen
as soon as	8.12	sobald	body	4.5	Körper
at least	8.11	mindestens	bomb	4.5	Bombe
at the back	7.2	hinten	book	3.4	reservieren, buchen
athlete	3.5	Athlet/in	boot	3.6	Stiefel
attendant	3.5	Aufseher/in	booth	Test 2	Kabine, (Telefon)zelle
aunt	2.4	Tante	bored	8.8	gelangweilt
Austrian	7.5	österreichisch; Österreicher/in	boring	4.2	langweilig
			borrow	8.2	sich leihen
auto	Test 4	Auto, PKW (US)	bowling	9.5	Bowling, Kegeln
awful	1.8	fürchterlich, furchtbar	box	8.1	Karton, Schachtel
			boyfriend	2.4	Freund
baby	8.1	Baby	bra	3.16	BH
bad throat	3.10	Halsschmerzen	Brazil	4.4	Brasilien
bake	4.3	backen	Brazilian	4.4	brasilianisch; Brasilianer/in
baked	3.17	gebacken			
baker's	7.2	Bäcker(laden)	break	5.3	Pause
			brother-in-law	2.1	Schwager

brush	6.1	bürsten	
build*	4.2	bauen	
bus stop	3.11	Bushaltestelle	
busy	3.10	beschäftigt	
butcher	3.5	Metzger/in	
cabbage	3.14	Kohl	
cake	6.5	Kuchen	
calculator	3.12	(Taschen)rechner	
call	6.5	Anruf	
calm	5.4	ruhig	
camcorder	3.13	Camcorder	
camera	3.6	Fotoapparat	
Canada	4.4	Kanada	
Canadian	4,4	kanadisch; Kanadier/in	
cap	3.16	Kappe, (Schild)mütze	
capital	9.5	Hauptstadt	
capital letter	1.2	Großbuchstabe	
car stereo	3.13	Stereo-Autoradio	
caravan	3.7	Wohnwagen	
card	6.1	Karte	
care	4.1	Sorgfalt, Vorsicht	
carefully	8.7	aufmerksam, genau	
carrot	3.14	Karotte	
cassette recorder	3.13	Cassettenrecorder	
catch*	1.3	erreichen	
cauliflower	3.17	Blumenkohl	
ceiling	Test 2	(Zimmer)decke	
central	4.2	zentral	
central station	3.4	Hauptbahnhof	
centre forward	3.6	Mittelstürmer/in	
check-in	1.8	Abfertigung	
cheer	5.1	jubeln, hurra rufen	
chemist's	7.2	Apotheke	
cherry	3.14	Kirsche	
children	5.2	Kinder	
China	4.4	China	
Chinese	4,4	chinesisch; Chinese, Chinesin	
chocolate	3.17	Schokolade	
Christmas Eve	3.2	Heiligabend	
cigar	9.2	Zigarre	
cigarette	9.2	Zigarette	
clarinet	3.6	Klarinette	
classical	3.6	klassisch	
cleaner	3.5	Reinemachefrau, "Putzmann"	
climb	6.4	(hoch)klettern	
climbing	Test 3	Klettern	
clock	3.12	Uhr	
cloud	8.13	Wolke	
clown	5.4	Clown	
coach	3.5	Trainer/in	
coach	3.7	Reisebus	
coin	3.12	Münze	
cold	3.10	Erkältung	
collect	4.2	sammeln	
collector	Test 3	Sammler/in	

come* down	8.2	herunterkommen	
come* over	1.8	herüberkommen	
comedy	3.6	Komödie	
comfortable	6.2	bequem	
company	8.10	Firma	
compose	4.5	komponieren	
composer	Test 3	Komponist/in	
composition	Test 3	Komposition	
computer game	8.10	Computerspiel	
concentrate	8.10	sich konzentrieren	
concert	2.1	Konzert	
condition	Test 3	Bedingung	
conductor	3.5	Schaffner/in	
contact lens	3.12	Kontaktlinse	
control	1.8	Kontrolle	
cook	3.5	Koch, Köchin	
cook	4.2	kochen	
cooker	9.2	Herd	
copy	1.5	Kopie	
correct	8.3	richtig	
cost*	5.4	kosten	
countryside	9.5	Landschaft, Gegend	
court	Test 1	Spielfeld, Platz	
cousin	2.1	Cousin/e	
cow	5.4	Kuh	
crash	9.5	einen Unfall haben mit	
crazy	1.8	verrückt	
credit card	3.7	Kreditkarte	
cross	3.4	überqueren	
crossing	3.11	Übergang	
cry	6.4	weinen	
cucumber	3.14	Salatgurke	
cupboard	Test 3	Schrank	
custom	6.6	Brauch, Tradition	
customer	3.5	Kunde, Kundin	
cutlet	3.17	Filet, Schnitzel	
cycling	3.15	Radfahren	
damaged	4.5	beschädigt	
dancer	2.4	Tänzer/in	
danger	1.5	Gefahr	
dangerous	9.5	gefährlich	
day return	7.2	Tagesrückfahrkarte	
decide	9.6	entscheiden	
delicious	1.7	köstlich, lecker	
department store	1.7	Warenhaus	
depend	8.10	abhängen	
desk	2.5	(Schul-)schreibtisch	
dessert	3.17	Nachspeise	
detective	2.4	Detektiv/in	
diamond	6.7	Diamant	
difference	6.6	Unterschied	
difficulty	6.5	Schwierigkeit	
direct	4.2	richten (auf)	
director	Test 3	Direktor/in	
dirty	1.9	schmutzig	
disagree	8.2	nicht übereinstimmen mit	
disco	6.2	Diskothek	
dish	Test 4	Schüssel	

98

distance	6.6	Entfernung	
dozen	3.1	Dutzend	
draw*	6.4	zeichnen	
dream	8.13	Traum	
dream*	8.13	träumen	
drive	8.13	Spazierfahrt	
driving test	8.8	Fahrprüfung	
drop	8.7	fallen lassen	
drums	2.1	Trommel	
Dutch	8.10	Holländer/in	
duty-free	1.8	zollfrei	
ear	5.1	Ohr	
eat* out	8.7	zum Essen ausgehen	
Ecuador	9.2	Ecuador	
elderly couple	1.8	älteres (Ehe)paar	
electric	4.2	elektrisch	
embarrass	4.1	verlegen machen	
employ	Test 5	beschäftigen, anstellen	
enemy	3.5	Feind/in	
engaged to	8.8	verlobt mit	
engineer	2.4	Ingenieur/in	
engineering	3.4	Maschinenbau	
enjoy	5.5	genießen	
enter	Test 1	hineingehen, betreten	
escape	8.10	ausbrechen	
exactly	1.8	genau	
example	1.3	Beispiel	
excite	4.1	aufregen	
excited	Test 5	aufgeregt, begeistert	
exercise	9.6	Übung	
exhausted	4.2	erschöpft	
exhibit	4.2	ausstellen	
exhibition	Test 3	Ausstellung	
expect	8.2	erwarten	
expression	8.6	Ausdruck	
extra	9.5	zusätzlich	
eye	7.2	Auge	
face	6.4	Gesicht	
factory worker	3.8	Fabrikarbeiter/in	
fair	5.3	blond, hell	
famous	1.9	berühmt	
fare	1.3	Fahrgeld, -preis	
fare	5.3	Flugpreis	
farmer	4.3	Bauer, Bäuerin	
fat	1.8	dick	
fault	4.5	Fehler	
faulty	Test 3	defekt	
favourite	8.9	Lieblings-	
female	9.2	weiblich	
ferry	3.9	Fähre	
festival	8.6	Fest	
file	3.12	(Akten)ordner	
final	8.3	letzte(r, s)	
finally	1.8	endlich, schließlich	
find*	1.8	finden	
fingernail	6.6	Fingernagel	
finish	8.2	beenden	

Finland	4.4	Finnland	
Finnish	4.4	finnisch	
fire	Test 4	Feuer, Brand	
first of all	1.8	als erstes, zunächst	
fishing	3.15	Fischen, Angeln	
flavour	9.7	Geschmack, Aroma	
flight	3.7	Flug	
flight attendant	1.8	Flugbegleiter/in	
florist	3.5	Blumenhändler/in	
fly*	1.8	fliegen	
(be*) fond of	8.8	gern mögen	
foot	8.1	Fuß	
football	1.4	Fußball	
for ages	8.11	Ewigkeiten	
for example	8.11	zum Beispiel	
forecast	6.7	Vorhersage	
foreigner	3.5	Ausländer/in	
forget*	8.2	vergessen	
France	4.4	Frankreich	
free kick	3.6	Freistoß	
freeze*	4.2	gefrieren	
freezing	8.3	eiskalt	
French	3.2	französisch	
French fries	3.17	Pommes frites	
fridge	9.2	Kühlschrank	
friendly	1.5	nett	
friendship	Test 4	Freundschaft	
(be*) frightened	9.6	Angst haben	
fun	4.1	Spaß	
funny	6.6	witzig, merkwürdig	
game	6.2	Spiel	
gas	4.2	Gas	
gentleman	8.1	Herr	
geography	2.5	Geography	
German	4.4	deutsch; Deutsche/r	
Germany	4.4	Deutschland	
get* down	Test 1	herunternehmen, -holen	
get* married	8.8	heiraten	
get* on	Test 1	weitermachen	
get* out	Test 1	aussteigen	
get* up	3.10	aufstehen	
gift	3.7	Geschenk	
girlfriend	2.4	Freundin	
give* in	Test 1	nachgeben	
give* up	1.7	aufgeben	
glove	5.4	Handschuh	
go* down	7.4	heruntergehen	
go* off	4.5	hochgehen	
go* up	8.2	hinaufgehen	
goal	9.2	Tor	
goal keeper	3.6	Torhüter/in	
golf	1.4	Golf	
granddaughter	2.4	Enkelin	
grandfather	2.4	Großvater	
grandmother	2.4	Großmutter	
grandson	2.1	Enkel	
grape	3.14	Weintraube	

Greece	4.4	Griechenland
Greek	4.4	griechisch; Grieche, Griechin
greengrocer's	7.2	Gemüseladen
grill	9.2	Grill
grilled	3.17	gegrillt
ground	6.7	(Erd)boden
guide book	3.7	Reiseführer
guitar	3.6	Gitarre
gun	1.8	Pistole
gym	3.4	Sporthalle
hairdo	4.1	Frisur
hairdresser	3.8	Friseur/in
hairdresser's	7.2	Friseur(salon)
hall	9.7	Halle
Halt!	9.7	Halt! Stop!
handbag	8.10	Handtasche
hang*	4.2	hängen
hanger	Test 3	(Kleider)bügel
happy	1.8	glücklich
harbour	4.1	Hafen
headache	3.10	Kopfschmerzen
headmistress	2.5	Schulleiterin
headphones	3.13	Kopfhörer
health	4.5	Gesundheit
heat	4.2	heizen
heavy rain	2.2	starker Regen
helicopter	8.9	Hubschrauber
help	8.13	Hilfe
hide*	9.3	verstecken
hire	3.9	mieten, leihen
hockey	9.2	Hockey
hold*	Test 3	halten
homework	1.4	Hausaufgaben
hopeless	5.3	hoffnungslos
horrible	8.13	fürchterlich
horse	4.2	Pferd
host	3.5	Gastgeber
hotel	7.2	Hotel
huge	8.3	riesig
Hungarian	4.4	ungarisch; Ungar/in
Hungary	4.4	Ungarn
hunger	3.10	Hunger
hurdle	8.4	Hürde
Hurry up!	1.2	Beeil dich!
hurry	1.7	sich beeilen
hurry	6.5	Eile
I used to live	9.6	früher wohnte ich
I'm a stranger here	3.5	ich bin hier fremd
I'm afraid	4.2	leider
icy	9.5	vereist, (spiegel)glatt
idea	3.10	Idee
identical	Test 4	identisch
identification	8.11	Ausweis
identify	Test 4	die Identität feststellen
identity	6.7	Identität
identity card	Test 4	Ausweis
illness	Test 3	Krankheit

immediately	8.7	sofort
improve	3.4	verbessern
in fact	8.11	eigentlich, tatsächlich
in love	8.11	verliebt
in time	1.8	rechtzeitig
independence	3.2	Unabhängigkeit
Indian	3.6	Indianer/in
inform	1.5	informieren
information	1.5	Information
insect	3.7	Insekt
inspect	4.3	kontrollieren, prüfen
inspector	Test 3	Inspektor/in
instruct	4.3	unterrichten, anweisen
instructor	3.5	Lehrer
instrument	9.2	Instrument
interest	4.1	Interesse
interested in	8.8	interessiert an
interesting	4.2	interessant
invitation	4.2	Einladung
invite	3.5	einladen
Ireland	4.4	Irland
Irish	4.4	irisch
jacket	3.16	Jacke, Jackett
Japan	4.4	Japan
Japanese	4.4	japanisch; Japaner/in
jeans	3.16	Jeans
joke	6.6	Witz
journalist	3.5	Journalist/in
journey	1.8	Reise
judo	9.2	Judo
jump	6.4	springen
jumper	3.16	Pullover
(be*) keen on	Test 5	sehr viel übrig haben für
keep* doing	8.11	immer wieder tun
keyboard	3.6	Keyboard
keyhole	8.4	Schlüsselloch
kick	6.4	kicken
kind	8.8	nett, freundlich
king	2.4	König
kiss	3.10	küssen
knee	9.2	Knie
knickers	3.16	(Damen)unterhose
knives	Test 2	Messer
knock	Test 3	klopfen
knock down	8.9	herunter-, umwerfen
lady	8.1	Dame
laid	5.4	gelegt
lamb	3.17	Lamm
lamp post	3.11	Laternenpfahl
land	8.2	landen
language	9.1	Sprache
laugh	8.2	lachen
lawyer	2.4	Rechtsanwalt, -anwältin
leaf	8.1	Blatt
leaves	5.2	Blätter
Lebanese	4.4	libanesisch; Libanese, Libanesin
Lebanon	4.4	Libanon

left	7.3	übrig	move	9.1	woanders hinstellen, umräumen
left-wing	4.5	politisch links stehend	mug	9.2	Kaffeebecher
lemon	3.14	Zitrone	murderer	8.10	Mörder/in
lemonade	2.2	Limonade	muscle	6.6	Muskel
lend*	4.3	leihen, verleihen	musical	9.2	Musik-
lense	3.4	(Kontakt)linse	musician	5.5	Musiker/in
lettuce	3.14	(grüner) Salat	nail	6.4	Nagel
librarian	3.8	Bibliothekar/in	nation	1.2	Nation
lie	Test 4	Lage, Position	national	3.2	National-
life	1.8	Leben	nationality	7.5	Nationalität
lighter	Test 4	Feuerzeug	nearly	3.3	fast
line	Test 1	Reihe, Schlange	need	9.1	brauchen
list	5.2	Liste	neighbour	8.6	Nachbar/in
litter bin	3.11	Abfallbehälter	nephew	2.1	Neffe
loaf	7.2	(Brot)laib	newsagent's	7.2	Zeitungskiosk
lobster	3.17	Hummer	niece	2.4	Nichte
lock	6.1	abschließen	noise	6.2	Geräusch
loo	3.11	Klo	noisy	1.8	laut
look after	3.5	sich kümmern um	normally	1.8	normalerweise
look for	Test 1	suchen	nose	9.2	Nase
lorry driver	3.8	Lkw-Fahrer/in	Not at all!	8.8	Bitte, gern geschehen!
lunch break	2.5	Mittagspause	note	3.12	Banknote
main course	3.17	Hauptgericht	note	8.9	Briefchen
main road	6.5	Hauptstraße	noun	1.2	Substantiv, Hauptwort
make* money	4.3	Geld verdienen	nurse	3.8	Krankenschwester, -pfleger
male	9.7	männlich			
manage	4.3	leiten	occasionally	8.7	gelegentlich
manager	2.4	Manager/in	of course	1.7	natürlich, selbstverständlich
map	9.1	Karte, Stadtplan			
marry	4.1	heiraten	office worker	3.8	Büroangestellte/r
mashed potato	3.17	Kartoffelbrei	officer	3.5	Beamter, Beamtin
match	2.2	Match	Olympic Games	3.2	Olympische Spiele
mathematics	2.5	Mathematik	Oman	4.4	Oman
mean*	1.8	bedeuten	Omani	4.4	omanisch; Omaner/in
meat	1.2	Fleisch	on foot	8.11	zu Fuß
mechanic	2.4	Mechaniker/in	on his own	8.11	ganz allein
medium	7.3	medium	one day	9.1	eines Tages
meet*	1.2	treffen	onion	3.14	Zwiebel
meeting	3.10	Besprechung, Treffen	opera	3.6	Oper
mess	8.12	Unordnung	opera singer	2.1	Opernsänger/in
Mexican	4.4	mexikanisch; Mexikaner/in	operate	4.3	bedienen, betätigen
			operator	Test 3	(Maschinen)arbeiter/in, Operator
Mexico	4.4	Mexiko			
midnight	8.6	Mitternacht	optician	3.4	Optiker/in
Midsummer('s Day)	8.6	Sommersonnenwende	orange	3.14	Orange
million	3.1	Million	orchestra	3.5	Orchester
minced	Test 3	gehackt	order	7.3	bestellen
mind	4.5	Geist, Verstand	organiser	8.11	Organisator/in
mineral	2.2	Mineral-	out of order	1.7	defekt
miss	1.8	verpassen	out of work	8.11	arbeitslos
mobile phone	3.13	Handy	over	8.4	über
moon	3.2	Mond	own	5.4	besitzen
mother-in-law	3.5	Schwiegermutter	owner	3.5	Besitzer/in
motorbike	3.11	Motorrad	paint	1.5	malen
mountain	6.4	Berg	painter	6.6	Maler/in
mousse	3.17	Mousse	pants	3.16	(Damen)unterhose
mouth	9.2	Mund	pants	Test 3	Hose
move	5.4	bewegen	paper	6.3	Zeitung

parents	2.1	Eltern		post office	7.2	Post(amt)
park	3.4	parken		poster	9.1	Poster, Plakat
Parliament	8.4	Parlament		potato	3.14	Kartoffel
part	9.2	Teil		powder	6.7	Pulver
pass a test	4.3	eine Prüfung bestehen		pram	3.11	Kinderwagen
				preposition	1.2	Präposition, Verhältniswort
pass the salt	7.1	das Salz reichen				
passenger	3.5	Passagier		priest	3.5	Priester
past	6.5	Vergangenheit		primary school	2.5	Grundschule
pavement	3.11	Gehweg		prince	2.4	Prinz
pea	3.14	Erbse		princess	2.4	Prinzessin
peach	3.14	Pfirsich		principal	3.5	Rektor
pear	3.14	Birne		principal	Test 4	hauptsächlich
penalty	3.6	Strafstoß, Elfmeter		prison	8.10	Gefängnis
permit	9.3	erlauben		problem	3.10	Problem
permitted	4.2	erlaubt		promise	8.13	Versprechen
personal CD	3.13	tragbarer CD-Player		promise	8.13	versprechen
personal stereo	3.13	Walkman		pronunciation	1.2	Aussprache
personality	6.6	Persönlichkeit		public toilet	3.11	öffentliche Toilette
pet	3.5	Haustier		purse	8.10	Portemonnaie
phone box	3.11	Telefonzelle		put* up	8.8	erhöhen
photocopier	8.8	Fotokopiergerät		quality	6.6	Qualität
photograph	5.5	Foto		queen	2.4	Königin
photography	3.6	Fotografie		queue	1.8	Schlange
phrasal verb	1.2	Verb mit Präposition		queue	8.13	Schlange stehen, anstehen
phrase	1.2	Satzteil				
physics	2.5	Physik		quiet	9.5	ruhig
piano	3.5	Klavier		really	8.7	wirklich
pie	3.17	Pastete		receptionist	2.4	Empfangsdame, -chef
pilot	2.4	Pilot/in		recommend	1.7	empfehlen
pineapple	3.14	Ananas		record	4.2	aufzeichnen
pipe	9.2	Pfeife		record	Test 2	(Schall)platte, Aufnahme
pitch	3.6	Platz, Feld				
pizza	6.3	Pizza		referee	2.2	Schiedsrichter/in
place	8.12	Ort		refuse	1.8	ablehnen
plan	8.13	Plan		remember	8.2	sich erinnern
plan	8.13	planen		remind	8.10	erinnern
plaster	3.7	Pflaster		rent	3.6	leihen, mieten
plastic	5.3	Plastik		report	4.3	berichten
pleased to meet you	7.5	freut mich, Sie / dich kennenzulernen		reporter	2.4	Reporter/in
				rest	6.5	Ruhepause
pleased	5.3	zufrieden		revolution	3.2	Revolution
pleasure	6.6	Vergnügen		rhyme	Test 3	sich reimen
plumber	3.8	Klempner/in		rich	1.9	reich
Poland	4.4	Polen		ride*	1.4	fahren
Polish	4.4	polnisch		rider	3.5	Reiter/in
politics	4.5	Politik		ridiculous	8.2	lächerlich
pool	1.5	Swimming Pool		riding	3.15	Reiten
poor	1.9	arm		ring	4.1	Ring
pop song	2.1	Popsong		ring*	9.4	anrufen, läuten
pork	3.17	Schweinefleisch		road sign	3.11	Straßenschild
port	3.7	Hafen		roast	3.17	(im Backofen) geröstet
porter	3.7	Portier				
Portugal	4.4	Portugal		route	5.4	Route
Portuguese	4.4	portugiesisch; Portugiese, Portugiesin		rubbish	Test 2	Abfall, Abfälle
				ruler	2.5	Lineal
				rump steak	3.17	Rumpsteak
possible	4.5	möglich		run*	4.3	laufen

English	Ref	German
runner	Test 3	Laufbursche, Bote, Botin
Russia	4.4	Rußland
Russian	4.4	russisch; Russe, Russin
safe	8.5	sicher
sailing	3.7	Segeln
sailor	3.8	Matrose
salad	3.17	Salat
salary	8.8	Gehalt
sale	9.7	Aus-, Schlußverkauf
salmon	3.17	Lachs
sandwich	3.10	Sandwich, belegtes Brot
saucer	4.5	Untertasse
scarf	3.16	Schal
schoolteacher	2.5	Lehrer/in
science	4	Naturwissenschaften
scientific	4	(natur)wissenschaftlich
scientist	4	(Natur)wissenschaftler/in
scissors	3.12	Schere
Scotland	4.4	Schottland
Scottish	3.17	schottisch
scream	1.8	schreien
season	8.6	Jahreszeit
seat	1.8	(Sitz)platz
second	3.1	zweite
secondary school	2.5	weiterführende Schule
serious	4.5	ernst
shake*	6.1	schütteln
shampoo	1.7	Shampoo
shine*	5.2	scheinen
shoot*	5.4	schießen
shop assistant	3.5	Verkäufer/in
short	1.9	klein
shorts	3.6	Shorts
shoulder bag	3.7	Umhängetasche
shout	5.4	rufen, schreien
shower	2.2	Schauer
shut	8.3	geschlossen
shut*	9.3	schließen
silly	6.2	dumm
single	7.2	Einzelfahrkarte
singular	Test 2	einzigartig, einmalig
sir	3.5	mein Herr
skating	3.15	Eislauf
skiing	3.7	Skilaufen
sleep*	9.3	schlafen
sleepy	1.9	schläfrig
slipper	9.2	Hausschuh
smart	2.2	schick, flott
smile	1.8	lächeln
sneeze	6.5	niesen
sock	2.2	Socke
sofa	2.1	Sofa
soldier	9.6	Soldat/in
sole	3.17	Seezunge
sore	8.1	weh, wund
sort	5.4	Sorte
sound	1.2	Klang
space	3.4	Platz
Spain	4.4	Spanien
Spanish	4.4	spanisch
spare time	4.3	Freizeit
special	3.2	besondere(r, s)
specialist	3.5	Spezialist/in
speed	6.6	Geschwindigkeit
spend*	9.3	ausgeben
spider	8.8	Spinne
sports club	5.3	Sportverein
stadium	2.2	Stadion
stamp	4.2	Briefmarke
stand* up	1.8	aufstehen
star sign	7.5	Sternzeichen
stare	4.1	starren
start	3.2	Beginn
starter	3.17	Vorspeise
starter	3.5	Starter/in, Teilnehmer/in
stay	Test 4	Aufenthalt
steak	5.1	Steak
stepfather	3.5	Stiefvater
steward	3.5	Flugbegleiter
stewardess	Test 1	Flugbegleiterin
stool	2.1	Schemel
store	3.5	Warenhaus
storm	4.1	Sturm
story	1.8	Geschichte
stranger	7.4	Fremde(r)
strawberry	8.1	Erdbeere
(be*) stuck	Test 1	festsitzen
stuff	Test 4	Zeug
stupid	1.4	dumm, blöd
subject	8.8	(Schul)fach
suddenly	1.8	plötzlich
suit	2.2	Anzug / Kostüm
sum	5.3	Rechenaufgabe
sun-bathing	3.7	Sonnenbaden
sunny	1.9	sonnig
sunshine	2.2	Sonnenschein
suntan lotion	3.7	Sonnenschutzmittel
surely	Test 2	bestimmt, sicher
surfing	3.15	Surfen
surprise	4.1	Überraschung
surprised	4.3	überrascht
sweater	3.16	Pullover
swim*	9.3	schwimmen
swimming	3.15	Schwimmen
Swiss	4.4	schweizerisch; Schweizer/in
switch off	9.6	ausschalten
switch on	9.5	an-, einschalten
Switzerland	4.4	die Schweiz

English	Ref	German
symbol	1.2	Symbol, Zeichen
symphony	3.6	Symphonie
system	Test 2	System
T-shirt	3.16	T-Shirt
table tennis	3.15	Tischtennis
Taiwan	4.4	Taiwan
Taiwanese	4.4	taiwanisch; Taiwaner/in
take*	9.6	dauern
talk	4.1	Gespräch
tape	3.6	Tonband
tasty	1.9	schmackhaft
tennis	3.15	Tennis
tennis court	2.2	Tennisplatz
tent	3.7	Zelt
terrible	1.7	schrecklich
(be*) terrified	9.6	schreckliche Angst haben
test	7.2	testen, prüfen
Thai	4.4	thailändisch; Thailänder/in
Thailand	4.4	Thailand
thick	6.6	dick, dicht
thief	8.10	Dieb/in
thin	1.8	dünn
thousand	3.1	tausend
throw*	5.4	werfen
tie	5.4	Krawatte, Schlips
tin	8.9	Dose
tire	4.1	ermüden
toast	5.1	Toast
toe	5.1	Zeh
tomato	3.14	Tomate
top	5.1	oberer Teil, Spitze
town hall	3.5	Rathaus
track-suit	3.16	Jogginganzug
traffic jam	1.8	Verkehrsstau
traffic lights	3.4	Verkehrsampel
trainers	3.16	Turnschuhe
translate	2.5	übersetzen
translator	Test 3	Übersetzer/in
travel bag	1.8	Reisetasche
traveller	1.8	Reisende(r)
traveller's cheque	3.7	Reisescheck
trout	3.17	Forelle
truth	6.1	Wahrheit
try	8.9	versuchen
tune	2.1	Melodie
tunnel	9.6	Tunnel
Turkey	4.4	Türkei
Turkish	4.4	türkisch
turn left / right	7.4	links / rechts abbiegen
twin room	3.7	Doppelzimmer mit 2 Einzelbetten
type	9.2	Art
uncle	2.1	Onkel
underpants	3.16	(Herren)unterhose(n)
unfortunately	8.7	leider
university	3.4	Universität
untidy	9.5	unordentlich
use	1.5	gebrauchen
useful	1.5	nützlich
useless	1.5	nutzlos
van	3.11	Lieferwagen
vegetarian	5.3	Vegetarier/in
verb	1.2	Verb, Zeitwort
vet	3.8	Tierarzt, -ärztin
Vietnam	4.4	Vietnam
Vietnamese	4.4	vietnamesisch; Vietnamese, Vietnamesin
view	6.6	Aussicht
violin	2.1	Geige
violinist	2.4	Geiger/in
visa	3.7	Visum
visit	8.13	Besuch
visitor	4.3	Besucher/in
vocabulary	3.4	Wortschatz
volleyball	2.2	Volleyball
vowel	1.3	Vokal, Selbstlaut
voyage	Test 2	Reise, Fahrt
Wales	4.4	Wales
walk	1.5	(zu Fuß) gehen
walk	8.11	Spaziergang
wall	1.5	Wand
wall	3.2	Mauer
wallet	3.12	Brieftasche
war	3.2	Krieg
washing-up	8.13	Abwasch
wasp	8.9	Wespe
weak	5.3	schwach
wear*	3.4	tragen
wedding	3.5	Hochzeit
weight	5.3	Gewicht
Welsh	4.4	walisisch
What a pity!	7.3	Wie schade!
What's the matter?	9.6	Was ist los?
wheel	9.2	Rad
widow	2.4	Witwe
windsurfing	3.15	Windsurfen
winner	3.5	Gewinner/in
wonder	4.1	Wunder
work	4.2	funktionieren
world	9.5	Welt
world war	3.2	Weltkrieg
worried	5.3	besorgt
worry	4.1	Sorge
worse	4.5	schlimmer
writer	3.5	Schriftsteller/in
yacht	3.7	Yacht
yoghurt	3.17	Joghurt
You're welcome!	7.4	Bitte, gern geschehen!
Zambia	9.2	Sambia